Rapid Ethnographic Assessments

This book provides a practical guide to understanding and conducting rapid ethnographic assessments (REAs) with an emphasis on their use in public health contexts. This team-based, multi-method, relatively low-cost approach results in rich understandings of social, economic, and policy factors that contribute to the root causes of an emerging situation and provides rapid, practical feedback to policy makers and programs.

Using real-world examples and case studies of completed REAs, Sangaramoorthy and Kroeger provide readers with a logical, easy-to-follow introduction into key concepts, principles, and methods of REAs, including interview and observation techniques, triangulation, field notes and debriefing, theoretical saturation, and qualitative analysis. They also provide a practical guide for planning and implementing REAs and suggestions for transforming findings into written reports and actionable recommendations. Materials and detailed tools regarding the conduct of REAs are designed to help readers apply this method to their own research regardless of topic or discipline. REA is an applied approach that can facilitate collaborative work with communities and become a catalyst for action.

Rapid Ethnographic Assessments will appeal to professionals and researchers interested in using REAs for research efficiency and productivity as well as action-oriented and translational research in a variety of fields and contexts.

Thurka Sangaramoorthy is a cultural and medical anthropologist and public health researcher with 22 years of expertise in conducting applied ethnographic research, including rapid assessments, among vulnerable populations in the United States, Africa, and Latin America/Caribbean. Her expertise includes global health and migration, HIV/STD, health systems, and environmental risk.

Karen A. Kroeger is a cultural and medical anthropologist who has conducted ethnographic research, assessment, and evaluation among populations vulnerable to sexually transmitted diseases and HIV in the United States and abroad since 1994. She is a former Research Anthropologist at the US Centers for Disease Control and Prevention (CDC).

Rapid Ethnographic Assessments

A Practical Approach and Toolkit For Collaborative Community Research

**Thurka Sangaramoorthy
and Karen A. Kroeger**

Routledge
Taylor & Francis Group

LONDON AND NEW YORK

First published 2020
by Routledge
2 Park Square, Milton Park, Abingdon, Oxon OX14 4RN

and by Routledge
52 Vanderbilt Avenue, New York, NY 10017

Routledge is an imprint of the Taylor & Francis Group, an informa business

British Library Cataloguing-in-Publication Data
A catalogue record for this book is available from the British Library

Library of Congress Cataloging-in-Publication Data
A catalog record has been requested for this book

ISBN: 978-0-367-25228-1 (hbk)
ISBN: 978-0-367-25229-8 (pbk)
ISBN: 978-0-429-28665-0 (ebk)

Typeset in Bembo
by Cenveo® Publisher Services

To Ashok, Gyan, and James—for the unwavering support
and enthusiasm that made this work possible.

—Thurka

To my mother, who awakened me at an early age to the notion that
there are worlds worth exploring beyond the one that I live in.

—Karen

Contents

Boxes

Figures

Tables

Preface

The journey for this book began a long time ago. We met in 2009 at the Centers for Disease Control and Prevention (CDC), when Thurka had the good fortune of working with Karen, then a research anthropologist in the Division of Sexually Transmitted Disease Prevention, during a postdoctoral fellowship in sexually transmitted disease (STD) prevention. As we began to work together, we discovered that we had a lot in common. Nearly a decade prior, Karen had completed the same postdoctoral fellowship. We were both trained in traditional cultural anthropology PhD programs, where we conducted long-term ethnographic fieldwork as lone anthropologists. We had similar research interests—Karen had conducted research on HIV risk among sex workers in Indonesia and had spent five years in CDC's Global AIDS Program working on programs for vulnerable populations. Thurka's research focused on the impact of HIV within Haitian communities and the effects of stigma on health and health outcomes among those living with HIV in urban settings.

We had also worked in public health contexts where we collaborated with interdisciplinary teams and communities to better understand the differential impacts of disease and plan effective interventions focused on health equity. Working in government public health, we often found ourselves walking a fine line between using the principles and methods of traditional ethnography and needing to generate timely information for action. We believed strongly in ethnography's power to bring depth and insight, but we were also distinctly aware of the confining realties that many public health programs face—depleted budgets, overworked staff, punishing bureaucratic deadlines, and, above all, the need to work quickly when facing disease outbreaks and other urgent problems.

We knew we were not alone in contemplating these challenges between traditional ethnography and its applied dimensions. Ethnography has a long and complex history of application in the federal government across multiple agencies (US General Accounting Office 2003). As early as 1852, Congress commissioned anthropologists to collect information on the social organization and relations of indigenous Native communities in the United States, and this analysis gave context and shape to policies which often had negative consequences on indigenous people (Baker 2010, Castile 2008). During the 1920s and the New Deal era, anthropologists in the US Department of Agriculture and the US Bureau of Agricultural Economics undertook a series of community studies to examine the cultures of rural agrarian communities in the US South in attempts to define poverty and develop instruments for its measurement (Adams 2007). These studies led to a series of policies and technical, institutional interventions focused on rural rehabilitation to solve the problem of rural poverty, including technical planning and bureaucratic supervision designed to maximize individual and community self-sufficiency (Baldwin 1968). During World War II and the post-war landscape, the United States began to emerge as a recognized global power, engaging in a period of global involvement. Anthropologists were instrumental to the reach of these global interventions, being tasked with teaching foreign service and military personnel regional culture, history, and language relevant to national defense and US participation in global affairs and engaging in research in the developing world (Borneman 1995).

Federal agencies have more recently used ethnographic methods to better understand and practically address programmatic issues or problems. A 2003 report on the use of ethnographic methods found that 10 federal agencies, ranging from the US Agency for International Development, the Environmental Protection Agency, and the Department of Health and Human Services used ethnographic methods in the past 15 years to assess the relationship between federal programmatic concerns and social lives of communities (US General Accounting Office 2003). The CDC, for instance, was noted to have employed rapid ethnographic assessment methods to examine populations experiencing high rates of sexually transmitted diseases to develop intervention strategies at the local level to reduce transmission. During the early-mid 2000s, CDC's Global AIDS Program supported rapid ethnographic assessments in Asia and Africa that helped lay the groundwork for HIV prevention and treatment programs serving vulnerable populations.

When Thurka joined the CDC, ethnographic efforts vis-à-vis rapid assessments were well underway in STD prevention efforts (Aral et al. 2005; Bloom et al. 2003). We worked together to develop, plan, and carry out several important rapid ethnographic assessments (REAs) on STD outbreaks and prevention. We also provided trainings on REAs to CDC staff, state and local health department personnel, and practitioners in non-governmental and community-based organizations from fields outside of public health. Even after Thurka took an academic position at the University of Maryland, we continued to collaborate on writing projects and training curriculums on REAs for academic researchers, practitioners, and students. We found that people were eager for methods that combined the emphasis of social-structural context in understanding events and meanings with the practical application of research in identifying, assessing, and mitigating problems. We began to think about how we could take what we had done at the CDC and beyond and share it with others interested in learning about rapid assessment methods. We also wanted to generate interest, support, and resources for qualitative social scientific research, work which is often undervalued and seen as marginal in many areas, including academic, government, non-profit, and other sectors. A publishing opportunity came up rather unexpectedly, and we felt strongly that writing a book in the vein of a toolkit was the best way to disseminate the usefulness of REAs widely.

This book is meant to serve as a practical guide to understanding and conducting REAs. REAs have a proven history of success in shifting policies and programmatic outcomes in health and development sectors where resources and local research capacity are often limited and where the success of interventions requires direct engagement and collaboration with local communities. Today, REAs have broad applicability for those interested in research efficiency and productivity as well as action-oriented and translational research—including students, researchers, and community members. Although we use examples from our own work in public health settings, our key objective is to demonstrate the increasing relevance of REAs for governments, non-governmental institutions and organizations, researchers, and communities in a variety of contexts. Researchers, program planners and staff, and policy-makers need practical research and assessment tools and skills that help them obtain timely information on emerging problems, engage local community members in problem solving, foster new collaborations, and inform program and policy adjustments. REAs are flexible and serve a variety of programmatic and policy needs including program planning, program evaluation, quantitative survey planning, and community participatory research.

REA, as applied knowledge, can also be a catalyst for theoretical development because it is inherently action-oriented, critical, and participative. It is decolonial in that it shifts the power dynamics away from longstanding norms in which dominant power structures of researchers, governments, and institutions determine research goals, practices, and parameters, with communities viewed as mere recipients. Instead, REA positions local actors in communities as equal partners by giving them the tools that facilitate self-determination and shared control of research, including the ethics of engagement, accountability, and presumed benefits. As a result, REAs aid in decision-making practices under real-life circumstances by engaging local communities in the research process as active participants and collaborators and center indigenous or local knowledge.

We have over 30 years of combined experience in conducting applied ethnographic and public health research, including large- and small-scale REAs related to health and well-being among vulnerable populations in the United States, Africa, and Asia. We both have a history of working in settings dominated by public health perspectives and quantitative methods as well as more traditional academic environments where applied and action-oriented research and researchers are often marginalized. We have demonstrated expertise in successfully navigating these settings and training academics and non-academics—students, faculty, public and community health professionals, social and health service providers in non-governmental organizations, and community members—in the design and conduct of REAs. Our combined experience working in domestic and international settings and across a variety of sectors means that we have a rich body of experience to draw on and the navigational skills to successfully emphasize the importance of community-driven participatory research. As such, we are uniquely positioned to bring a set of perspectives and experiences to our book that differentiates it from those that currently exist on rapid assessment methods, applied qualitative research, and ethnographic methods.

Our book can serve as the main textbook in courses or training programs where the emphasis is on applied qualitative research. It can also serve as a supplementary textbook in courses or training programs focused on research methods in a variety of disciplines (e.g., anthropology, sociology, communication, public health, education, urban planning, etc.), as well as general courses in the fields of global health, public health, health policy and administration, and anthropology. We are also committed to writing in a manner that is accessible, usable, and helpful to those outside the academy—community leaders, program managers, field staff, program consultants, and scientific staff. We envision our audience as including scholars and practitioners in low- and middle-income countries or low-resource settings where research capacity is still growing and the need for response to problems is urgent. We are confident that this book is essential reading for researchers interested in collaborating with communities to provide rapid collection and dissemination of information useful for key decision makers utilizing ethnographic and qualitative methods.

References

Adams, Jane. 2007. Ethnography of rural North America. *North American Dialogue* 10(2): 1–6.

Aral, Sevgi, Janet St.Lawrence, Roman Dyatlov, and Andrei Kozlov. 2005. Commercial sex work, drug use, and sexually transmitted infections in St. Petersburg, Russia. *Social Science & Medicine* 60(10): 2181–2190.

Baker, Lee D. 2010. *Anthropology and the Racial Politics of Culture*. Durham, South Africa: Duke University Press.

Baldwin, Sidney. 1968. *Poverty and Politics: The Rise and Decline of the Farm Security Administration*. Chapel Hill, NC: University of North Carolina Press.

Bloom, Frederick, Kata Chillag, and Mary Yetter. 2003. Philadelphia's Syphilis outbreak in gay men: an application of rapid ethnographic assessment for public health in the U.S. *Practicing Anthropology* 25(4): 28–32.

Borneman, John. 1995. American anthropology as foreign policy. *American Anthropologist* 97(4): 663–672.

Castile, George Pierre. 2008. Federal Indian policy and anthropology. In *A Companion to the Anthropology of American Indians*, edited by Thomas Biolsi, pp. 268–283. Maiden, MA: Blackwell.

United States General Accounting Office. 2003. *Federal Programs: Ethnographic Studies Can Inform Agencies' Actions: Staff Study*. Washington DC: US General Accounting Office.

Chapter summaries

In Chapter 1, "Overview of rapid ethnographic assessment," we introduce readers to the REA method. We discuss the purpose and provide the defining characteristics and theoretical frameworks constituting REAs. We also include a discussion of when REAs are useful and under which circumstances they are not appropriate. Further, we provide the reader with an overview of REA, its history, and examples of its use in various contexts and disciplines. Finally, we discuss the basic principles underlying anthropological methods and theories as well as the orientations of qualitative, applied, and action-oriented research and their positioning within disciplines with a strong focus on "evidence-based research."

In Chapter 2, "Key considerations in planning for a rapid ethnographic assessment," we outline key concepts and considerations of REAs. Specifically, we detail the kinds of questions a REA is best designed to address and whether REAs are applicable and appropriate for certain types of research or programmatic questions. Further, we consider decisions related to the design and scope of the REA. We also discuss the various types of expertise (e.g., technical, lay, etc.) needed, the time and resource commitments required, and the types of dissemination plans of REA findings to consider. We focus on the roles of local, community stakeholders, including the role of community members in identifying study objectives and selecting appropriate study designs. Finally, we discuss the role of funding and funders (e.g., government, non-profit, etc.) and the complexity of data ownership. We contend that these issues are particularly important for those who are located outside the academy (i.e., communities) as it may have serious implications for data ownership, retention, and access. We also offer sample budget items.

In Chapter 3, "Rapid ethnographic assessment design and methods," we discuss issues specific to the design and conduct of REAs, including constructing and conceptualizing key aims and objectives; sampling frames; methods such as ethnographic observation, ethnographic and geospatial mapping, in-depth key informant interviews, focus groups, and surveys; and writing field notes. We also provide a practical guide to the advantages and challenges of certain methods as well as suggestions for using several combinations of methods depending on the scale and scope of the research.

In Chapter 4, "Fieldwork," we illustrate the fundamentals of team-based fieldwork. We discuss critical questions of how to choose team members with a particular emphasis on disciplinary skill sets and orientations. REAs can be catalysts for community collaborations; therefore, we attend to the issue of skills transfer and the potential for building research and assessment capacity in communities where research is not the norm and data may not be readily available. We also include a thorough discussion of how to plan and proceed with team debriefings. Further, we review issues related to field safety with practical considerations for understanding issues related to gendered, racial, ethnic, and power dynamics of fieldwork. Finally, we consider ethics in various dimensions including research values; informed consent; confidentiality; accountability and responsibility to participants, collaborators, and the public; and common ethical dilemmas and conflicts that arise in team-based community-driven participatory research.

In Chapter 5, "Data analysis," we provide an in-depth overview and practical step-by-step instructions on qualitative data management, qualitative data analysis, and triangulation. We specifically detail practical and logistical issues related to rapid data analysis including the construction of the aims and objectives of analysis, analytical styles, data preparation and management in team-based research, issues of reliability and validity, and computer-based qualitative analysis software. We also critically discuss the composition of the analytical team and considerations for including and engaging community members in the process of data analysis and preliminary findings.

In Chapter 6, "Report writing and follow up," we detail how to construct and present key findings and outcomes especially to decision makers, program administrators, and policy makers. We provide specific instruction on writing clear and concrete recommendations for a variety of audiences, developing a dissemination plan for findings, and creating a follow-up plan for addressing further needs. We discuss the potential challenges and solutions related to community-driven research that may arise during the analytical and dissemination phases.

In Chapter 7, "Case studies," we provide rich, comprehensive information on three case studies of REAs we planned and conducted. We select these case studies to illustrate the range, size, and scope of REAs, including small and large REAs and US- and internationally-based REAs, reflecting both jurisdictional as well as cross-cultural parameters related to scale that need critical consideration.

In the appendices section we include additional, essential materials and information, including a glossary of terms, sample budget, and project planning tool and additional resources such as weblinks and references. This section also serves as the basis for materials to be included in a companion website for students and instructors.

Acknowledgments

It takes an entire community to write a book. Although getting thoughts and words to the computer screen is a fairly solitary endeavor, the ideas and experiences that lead to the words which eventually transforms into a book takes a community of people. We are both deeply indebted to a number of individuals and institutions for the support and resources we have received in bringing this book to press.

We would like to thank the many people at the Centers for Disease Control and Prevention (CDC), the various Ministries of Health and US-based state health departments, the University of Maryland, and those involved in REA projects globally and in the United States who helped shape the content and form of this practical guide through their involvement and participation in different stages of its development.

Thurka is particularly grateful for the continued support of students and colleagues at the University of Maryland, especially the friendship, support, and encouragement received from Erica Glasper Andrews, Lynn Bolles, Stephen Brighton, Typhanye Dyer, Christina Getrich, Emilia Guevara, Kimberly Griffin Hayes, Amelia Jamison, Nipun Kottage, Andrea López, Mona Mittal, Helen Mittmann, Sybil Paige, Devon Payne-Sturges, Samantha Primiano, and Joe Richardson during this process. This book also could not have been completed without a full-year sabbatical made possible through generous financial support from the Graduate School's Research and Scholarship Award, the Office of Faculty Affairs, the College of Behavioral and Social Sciences, and the Department of Anthropology. Gregory Ball, Wayne McIntosh, and Paul Shackel were instrumental in providing time and resources needed to write and publish this book.

Colleagues at the CDC within the National Center for HIV/AIDS, Viral Hepatitis, Sexually Transmitted Diseases, and Tuberculosis Prevention were critical to conversations related to the intersections of ethnography and public health prevention methods. Fred Bloom, Hazel Dean, Kathleen McDavid Harrison, Matthew Hogben, David Johnson, Tanya Telfair, Penny Loosier, Donna McCree, Eleanor McLellan, Greg Millet, Ramal Moonesinghe, Ranell Myles, Thomas Painter, Laurie Reid, Rebecca Schmidt, Madeleine Sutton, Jo Valentine, Petra Vallila-Buchman, Kim Williams, and Samantha

Williams were amazing colleagues who made interdisciplinary and interprofessional collaboration meaningful and empowering.

Finally, the support of family and friends was crucial to the development and completion of this book. Long-time writing partners and friends, Adia Benton and Jennifer Liu, provided thoughtful feedback on earlier versions of the manuscript, while the Cerwinski and Sangaramoorthy families helped out with childcare and other forms of invisible labor that made writing possible. Ashok, Gyan, and James Cerwinski, in particular, proved to be the most enthusiastic cheerleaders anyone could ask for.

Karen would like to acknowledge several colleagues at the CDC, including Fred Bloom, a fellow anthropologist, who helped make the transition to CDC in 2001 particularly welcoming. Fred's wise counsel, unfailing good humor, and friendship helped ground the years at CDC. Rich Needle and Naomi Bock in the Global AIDS Program provided important opportunities to collaborate on large-scale REAs and work with vulnerable populations. Eleanor McLellan's collegiality, patience with questions, attention to detail, and depth of methodological knowledge improved every manuscript, training session, and protocol.

Rapid ethnographic assessment has always been a bit of an outlier at the CDC, but Rich Needle, Fred Bloom, Janet St. Lawrence, Sevgi Aral, and Matthew Hogben, in particular, gave unstinting support for the approach. Over the years, many CDC public health fellows and colleagues put in tireless hours of work on every aspect of REAs. They are too numerous to mention by name, but they know who they are and their contributions are immeasurable. Their questions helped spur mutual learning that led to improvements in training for and implementing REAs. The Global AIDS program offered opportunities to collaborate with and learn from talented country nationals implementing REAs, including Judite Langa at CDC-Mozambique and Charles Parry at the Medical Research Council in South Africa.

Writing is a solitary exercise, even when undertaken in partnership. Family and friends in far-flung places gave enthusiastic support and were a welcome distraction at moments when it was sorely needed, especially Diana Gores, Sarah Sbarra, Jennifer Gores, Russ Kroeger, Catherine Koziol, Alice Klement, Mary Williams, Lucy Moorman, Jeri Malone, Lorrie Burroughs, Ann Temkin, and Elaine Wesley. Without them, the hours at the computer would have seemed much longer.

Collectively, we would like to thank Adia Benton, Jennifer Liu, and Andrea López for taking the time to meticulously review the book proposal and Chapter 1. Their generous comments helped us formulate clear goals and objectives for this book. Moreover, we would be remiss if we did not acknowledge those who have participated in our various REA workshops and trainings. We have benefitted immensely from their feedback and active engagement. Students in Thurka's Qualitative Methods in Applied Anthropology class at the University of Maryland over the years also provided invaluable assistance in helping us think through the benefits of this method to a wide audience.

We would like to thank Hannah Shakespeare for being a supportive editor as well as Matt Bickerton and the rest of the staff at Routledge and Apoorva Mathur and the staff at Cenveo Publisher Services for seeing this book through to publication. The comments we received from external reviewers and copy editors were extremely valuable and helped make important improvements to the book. The final manuscript benefitted tremendously from the diligent work of Ellen Platts, who provided instrumental assistance with formatting, and Sarah Ahmed, who supported us in finalizing our resource guide.

Finally, we would like to thank the following individuals and institutions for their permission to use tables and figures. Maya Kearney, Evelyn Lopez, Stephanie Madden, Janna Napoli, and Søren Peterson for allowing us to use their figure "Mind Map of Safety Resources and Services;" Caitlin Cromer, Charlene Gatewood, and Yurong He for letting us reprint the observational maps in their paper "Understanding Diversity on McKeldin Mall;" and Jossey-Bass for permission to use Table 3.1: Style of Data Collection from *Qualitative Methods in Public Health: A Field Guide for Applied Research* by Priscilla R. Ulin, Elizabeth T. Robinson, and Elizabeth E. Tolley.

We wish to make clear that the findings and conclusions in this book are our own, and do not represent the official position of the Centers for Disease Control and Prevention.

1 Overview of rapid ethnographic assessment

Key learning outcomes

1 Identify key concepts and principles of rapid ethnographic assessment (REA)
2 Understand how REA relates to other qualitative and community-engaged participatory research approaches
3 Know when REA may be useful and when it is not

What influences women in Mexico City to breastfeed their infants? What motivates Native American gay, bisexual, and transgender men to use or not use available HIV prevention services? What factors limit children's access to quality primary education in the Kakuma refugee camp in Kenya? How is tourism development affecting residents in communities along Camino Real de Tierra Adentro, a historic trail between Mexico and the United States?

Although traditional qualitative and quantitative studies may answer questions like these, such research can often take months or even years to design and implement. They can also consume considerable resources before findings are finalized and shared. Program managers and practitioners in public health, education, and other fields often need to act quickly to make decisions about how well programs are working and what needs to be changed or adjusted to help them to better reach, serve, and respond to the needs of their clients. The need for timely, useable data can be especially critical for programs serving socially marginalized or vulnerable populations because these populations are often hidden, hard to reach, and geographically mobile due to a variety of social, political, and environmental factors. In the current social and political environment, program planners and staff as well as policymakers often find themselves needing practical research and assessment tools and skills that help them obtain timely information on emerging problems, engage local community members in problem solving, foster new collaborations, and inform program and policy adjustments. In this book, we share our experience with REA, a practical, applied method and approach for quickly obtaining community-level data that researchers, program planners and managers, students, and community members can use to understand and alleviate problems.

We broadly define vulnerable populations as social or demographic groups that have relatively limited access to necessary social, political, and economic resources. Vulnerable populations can include persons who lack access to the traditional means of power and experience marginalization due to economic, racial, and gender disparities. Vulnerable populations may also include those who are unstably housed or homeless; uninsured or under-insured; chronically ill or disabled; and the working poor. They can be persons involved in stigmatized or criminalized behaviors such as illicit drug use, sex work, or same-sex relationships. Other populations, such as migrant workers and refugees, may also be vulnerable because they are highly mobile and hard to reach due to seasonal work, war, or environmental disasters. Vulnerable populations often lack access to important social and health services because of social, institutional, policy, and personal barriers. They may not use available services due to stigma, discrimination, and fear of arrest or deportation.

Over the past decade, programs that serve vulnerable populations have had to innovate and adapt quickly to new conditions brought about by severe budget cuts to public health and social services, rapid shifts in social welfare and development priorities, and increasing social, economic, and health disparities. Many programs have had to develop new, more sustainable models of care and engagement for the communities that they serve. This often requires engaging directly with community members to understand their perspectives and involving them in the search for potential solutions.

This community-driven research orientation, which is central to the approach described in this book, places the "insider perspective" at the heart of any research or assessment question. It also presumes that community members have substantial insight into problems and that engaging community members as part of the research process will result in more feasible, practical solutions.

In this book we lay out the theoretical orientation and principles of REA, an applied research method that we have used in our own research, teaching, and community engagement work. We demonstrate how the concepts and practices incorporated in this approach have been used in a variety of domestic and international settings and serve both programmatic and policy needs.

In writing this book, we have made a conscious decision to use the term "REA" to describe the approach we have used in our work. As anthropologists, we are well aware of debates in our discipline regarding whether rapid approaches can be sufficiently "ethnographic." As researchers, we have conducted more traditional anthropological research in the form of long-term ethnographies, where we spent months and years in the field. We have a keen understanding of what is gained and what is lost in these two very different approaches. We firmly believe that, skillfully applied, it is possible to undertake short-term, rapid research that remains grounded in ethnographic principles. We contend that by using this term, and by emphasizing the centrality of an ethnographic orientation to the work, we are able to engage more effectively with others not trained in anthropology or ethnographic methods about the advantages of using anthropological approaches.

By suggesting that our book would be beneficial to those outside the discipline of anthropology and academic settings, we do not imply that REA and applied research are of lesser importance to those within the discipline or the academy. There is deep anthropological and academic value in applied work, and the lessons learned from REA significantly contribute to the discipline and the training of students in academic programs, the majority of whom are eventually employed outside the academy (Gupta and Ferguson 1997). As we explain below, throughout this book we take seriously the theoretical significance of practice—ideas that clarify and justify the role of practice within and outside the discipline—that focuses on community-driven acquisition of knowledge and its utilization. Thus, we embrace societal or community problem solving as a mainstream disciplinary pursuit, one that contributes to the development and advancement of anthropological theory (Baba 2000). REA is an approach and orientation that illustrates the interdependence of knowledge and action and proves itself capable of producing rigorous problem-oriented scholarship.

What is REA?

REA is primarily a qualitative research method that focuses on the collection and analysis of locally relevant data. It is an approach and orientation to data collection that can be used for a variety of purposes; for example, for exploratory or formative research, for program assessment or needs assessment, as a rapid response tool, or for program evaluation. REA is used to elicit rich description about the context in which things occur, and about processes, systems, motivations, and relationships. REAs often allow research teams to assess a variety of complex social and structural issues to improve programs and policies impacting marginalized and vulnerable populations.

REAs mainly rely on qualitative data collection methods such as interviews and focus groups but also incorporate other methods such as structured observations, mapping, and short surveys. They draw on principles of ethnography, an approach used historically by anthropologists, to learn about the social and cultural conditions of individuals and communities. The primary goal of ethnography is to understand a problem or situation from the perspective of the "insider," whether the insider is a health provider in a clinical setting, an outreach worker, or a community member who lives in a neighborhood experiencing disease increases. As some anthropologists have described it, the purpose of ethnography is to understand another way of life from the perspective of those who have experienced it, and to "learn from" rather than "study" people (Spradley 1980).

A fundamental aspect of anthropological research is the integration of "emic" or insider perspectives (i.e., perspective of the subject) with "etic" or external perspectives (i.e., perspective of the observer). Incorporating these perspectives in a holistic approach usually results in findings and recommendations that are based on detailed and culturally rich information and grounded in local realities. However, unlike more traditional qualitative research methods, REAs emphasize information for action, which is achieved through a few key principles: (1) the rapid collection and dissemination of information useful for key decision makers; (2) the use of multidisciplinary assessment teams; and (3) triangulation across multiple data collection methods and sources to strengthen the validity of findings, which are aimed at developing practical, achievable recommendations. REA is oriented toward rapid response and carried out over a relatively compressed period of time, with data collection usually taking several days to several weeks, depending upon the scope, and up to several months for analysis of data and report writing. Because of its limited scope, REA is typically less expensive to undertake than other types of studies.

REAs have often been used in health and development sectors where resources and local research capacity are often limited, and where the success of interventions requires direct engagement and collaboration with local communities. In some situations, REA has created a framework for communities to work together to address a need or problem and as a means of transferring research skills to local communities. Today, REAs have broad applicability for anyone interested in research efficiency and productivity as well as action-oriented and translational research.

We intend for this book to be useful to students, researchers, community advocates, public health practitioners, urban planners, and education specialists—many of whom have worked for years to improve programs and policies that impact marginalized and vulnerable populations. In addition, we hope the book appeals to academics in the social sciences, public health, communication, urban development, education, and other fields, who are training future generations of students and researchers interested in doing practical, applied work.

REA in the context of community-engaged research

REA, like other rapid data collection methods, has deep roots in international health and development, arising in the 1970s from a need to respond quickly to problems in communities where few data were available. Reasons for this absence of data varied. Developing countries or communities often lacked disease surveillance or other types of systems infrastructure to collect data, and few had economic or human resources needed to carry out studies to gather information on a large scale. In some cases, a problem was new or emerging, so data were non-existent. Development experts in agriculture, community development, and health, many of whom were trained social scientists, realized there was a need to innovate. They sought a middle ground between "quick and dirty" methods such as cursory observations made by external professionals during site visits and, at the other extreme, traditional social science studies such as long-term ethnography or surveys that could take years to complete and result in few data that could be applied to planning programs and services. Approaches such as Rapid Rural Appraisal (Chambers 1979) developed, in which teams of researchers worked alongside local people and employed a variety of qualitative and observational methods including individual and group interviews, field observations and ethnographic mapping, archival study, and rapid, street-based surveys and censuses to quickly obtain information related to a focused problem or question.

Over the years, numerous models developed that were similar to Rapid Rural Appraisal. These approaches drew on anthropological principles of "treating [insiders] as teachers" (Chambers 1979), and sought to reverse existing social and intellectual hierarchies that positioned the researcher (or outsider) as the expert and community members as subjects of research. Health and development workers recognized that drawing on indigenous knowledge, practices, and experiences in program design could determine their success or failure. This shift toward a more participatory and engaged view of local populations, which placed the researcher in the position of "learner," coincided with a reflexive turn in anthropology, which overlapped with a broader social revolution related to civil rights, women's liberation, and anti-war sentiment that was occurring in the 1960s and 1970s in the United States and beyond. During this period, anthropology as a discipline was in the process of reinventing itself (Hymes 1969).

For much of its history, anthropology was organized around the study of the "savage slot," examining the everyday life of so-called primitive, small-scale, or savage societies disempowered by Western colonial powers (Trouillot 2003). Anthropologists themselves often worked for colonial powers that used their research on local customs to subdue and exploit indigenous populations. In the mid-twentieth century, however, anthropologists began to acknowledge that research itself was a form of "scientific colonialism," a process driven by the interests of the powerful and wealthy that seldom benefitted the communities being studied (Galtung 1967). Encouraged to "study up" (Nader 1969) and decolonize (Harrison 1997), many in the discipline sought to examine the people who wielded power and the structures that maintained them. In coming to terms with the uses and abuses of their work, anthropologists also began to better clarify ethnographic practice and fieldwork to a broader audience, often challenging the singular authority of the researcher and approaching research as collaborative, activist engagements (Fals Borda 2001; Reiter and Oslender 2014). Outside of anthropology, other fields like education were also being influenced by rapid cultural changes, shifting toward a more participatory, action-oriented, and decolonizing approach inspired by the work of Brazilian educator Paulo Freire (2006), among others.

Over the next few decades, rapid data collection models proliferated into a veritable "alphabet soup" of labels and acronyms, often captured under

Table 1.1 Examples of rapid research methods

Approach	Acronym	Reference	Field
Rapid Rural Appraisal	RRA	Chambers 1979	Agriculture
Participatory Rural Appraisal	PRA	Chambers 1994	Community Development
Rapid Assessment Program	RAP	Parker III and Bailey 1991	Biological Conservation
Rapid Assessment Procedures	RAP	Scrimshaw and Gleason 1992	Health and Nutrition
Rapid Anthropological Assessment	RAA	Manderson 1996	Health
Rapid Assessment Process	RAP	Beebe 2001	International Development
Rapid Assessment and Response	RAR	Fitch and Stimson 2003	Global Public Health
Rapid Assessment Response and Evaluation	RARE	Trotter et al. 2001	Public Health

the general rubric of "assessment" but employing other similar labels such as "appraisal," "procedures," or "process" (see Table 1.1). The history of these approaches—their developmental "family tree"—along with their similarities and differences, has been well-covered elsewhere (Beebe 2001, 2014). However, most of these approaches adhere to similar core principles— research driven by the need for timely data to be used for practical purposes. This usually means that there is a focused research question and a relatively short period of data collection. Data are collected by a multidisciplinary team of researchers, often working in concert with local people. Although not all models rely exclusively on the collection of qualitative data, the majority center on interviews that draw on indigenous or local knowledge as the core component of the data collection process. These approaches have been used in numerous fields, including agriculture, community development, environmental and natural resource management, education, and policy. In health, they have been used to develop or evaluate programs for waterborne diseases, HIV and other sexually transmitted infections, women's reproductive health, and substance abuse, among other needs.

The proliferation of these rapid data collection methods, particularly those that rely on ethnographic data collection and analysis techniques, suggests that ethnography as it has been traditionally conceived is being re-interpreted and re-oriented towards practice that has direct benefits to the communities involved. Further, it also indicates that ethnographic methods are increasingly being taken up and adopted by researchers in a variety of fields beyond anthropology (e.g., education, sociology, public health, urban studies, journalism) making it useful in a variety of contexts and applicable to a variety of research questions. Our goal is to demonstrate the usefulness of REA as a tool that not only benefits communities, researchers, policy makers, and programs, but also advances anthropology's commitment to ameliorating contemporary social problems.

Moreover, REA fits within the rubric of a long tradition of community-based participatory research (CBPR), known for its equity-focused approach to health research. In CBPR, research is conceptualized as an inherently collaborative process between researchers, communities, and other stakeholders to leverage data and build on existing strengths and priorities of communities in order to improve health equity. CBPR can occur in varied contexts, from clinical trials to basic community-level data collection. Further, the methods and tools used can encompass a wide range of qualitative and quantitative methods. Although projects undertaking CBPR approaches are incredibly diverse, common factors that unite them include how research is conducted, how different constituents are involved, and how work is presented and used (Israel et al. 2010; Minkler and Wallerstein 2011). CBPR has been institutionalized in many sectors, especially public health, yet questions of research rigor, validity, and value, as well as conflicts that arise within the context of collaboration remain common challenges.

Ultimately, we see REA as a method that can be used to support and inform various models of rapid and community-based participatory research. We understand that while some of the principles and methods of REA have been used by non-anthropologists, an ethnographic orientation or sensibility toward local knowledge or social hierarchies may not have been fully incorporated. We think we can help readers better understand how this orientation differs from other forms of research, and how it can help to inform and enrich CBPR, community-based needs assessments, and other similar methods.

Despite the proliferation and use of rapid data collection methods for various purposes, the results of these approaches are seldom published. Consequently, rapid assessment methods are not being shared widely with those who might wish to undertake similar work. In some cases, sponsors (e.g., governments, international institutions, and corporations) impose classified and restricted access agreements that limit the circulation of reports or documents to funders and other key stakeholders. In part, this may be due to a perceived lack of impact or interest in the results of assessments, which are often used for practical purposes and not viewed as generalizable. As a result, this work often circulates internally within an organization or appears only in the gray literature, which makes it difficult to find and locate. Consequently, because their findings and methods are rarely disseminated on the scale of traditional academic peer-reviewed publications, many researchers have not heard of rapid assessment approaches or do not understand them well.

Even when those conducting rapid assessments try to publish their work in peer-reviewed journals, they face considerable challenges. Some publishing venues have a tendency to reject qualitative research papers on methodological grounds, often arguing that such studies are of low priority, lacking in practical value, insufficiently theoretical, unlikely to be highly cited, or not of interest to readers (Greenhalgh et al. 2016). These challenges are not unique to those who conduct REAs, as they impact qualitative researchers more broadly. Such rejections, even if discouraging, can be opportunities to educate those who may not have training in reading or evaluating qualitative studies. As we argue later in the book, certain research questions such as those pertaining to socio-political context, program or policy translation, social interactions, and community perspectives are best answered by qualitative studies. Good qualitative research with well-defined, focused results can be popular with readers, highly cited, and advance knowledge.

REAs can also face unique publishing challenges even in venues where qualitative research is widely published. Critics feel that work utilizing rapid qualitative data collection methods lack rigor or that the findings of such work are insufficiently theoretical and of little interest to audiences accustomed to more traditional types of studies. Despite criticism from traditional methodologists and ethnographers (who are often located within the academy) about questions related to reliability and validity due to its relatively rapid nature, essential ethnographically rich data based on community-driven needs can be collected within the realities of programmatic time and budgetary constraints. Our understanding and practice of ethnography does not limit it to a particular method (i.e., participant observation—the cornerstone of traditional ethnography) or specific way of generating knowledge (i.e., long-term immersion). For us, ethnography is also a kind of sensibility that prioritizes understanding how people make sense of their social and material realities (Schatz 2009). Ethnography, when envisioned in this way, is more than an on-site data collection process. It is an epistemological commitment to community perspectives and needs, using multiple tools of inquiry that are flexible and necessary for studying the contemporary social world.

Throughout the book, we show how REAs can complement data collection and analytical approaches traditionally used in anthropology and public health such as long-term ethnography or focus groups, reconfiguring them in new and innovative ways. REAs emphasize the importance of applied knowledge as a foundation for theoretical development through the conduct of research that is applied, action-oriented, critical, and decolonial. Often, dominant and powerful constituents such as researchers, governments, or institutions determine research goals and objectives, without consideration of ethics, accountability, or unequal power dynamics embedded within research itself (Smith 2012). The use of REAs can provide local actors and communities with the tools needed to shift this process of knowledge production to center on the attainment of community-driven goals, facilitating self-determination and shared control of the research process as well as the ethics of engagement. As a result, REAs aid in decision-making practices under real-life circumstances by engaging local communities in the research process as active participants and collaborators and centering indigenous or local knowledge. REAs, therefore, represent an equity-driven approach to research that can be exceedingly useful. With appropriate guidance and leadership, implementation of successful REAs can be carried out with minimal research training. At a moment when traditional

---

Box 1.1

Example: Need more information

Epidemiologic data indicate that HIV disproportionately affects Native American gay and bisexual men, yet little is known about why the risk of acquiring HIV has increased among this population. Researchers wanted to gather more information about Native American men who have same-sex experiences. The use of REA methodology allowed for culturally sensitive, community-driven research to gather more information about these sensitive and stigmatized topics. The study identified several factors that could increase HIV risk among Native American gay and bisexual men such as mistrust of HIV service organizations, barriers to obtaining condoms, and easy availability and access to casual sex interactions (i.e., "hookups").

Adapted from Burks et al. 2011

---

ethnography is being reconceived and ethnographic methods are increasingly being employed by non-anthropologists (LeCompte 2002; Bejarano et al. 2019), we provide a guide that demonstrates both the applied and theoretical significance of REAs in the contemporary social and political landscape.

When is REA useful?

It is important to know when and when not to use REA and to plan and prepare accordingly. REA is very useful in a number of contexts. First, it is useful when we need more information about a problem (see Box 1.1). Often, there are problems where very little is known or situations that are poorly understood. REAs elicit rich, descriptive information that contributes to understanding why a problem or a situation may be occurring and how best to respond. REAs help program managers obtain information about individual and community perceptions, beliefs, motivations, and practices that affect both longstanding and emergent problems. For instance, REAs can help to understand factors that contribute to increases in disease and the social and environmental context in which increases occur, as well as structural or systemic factors that affect how people access and use health services.

Second, REA is useful when the problem may be developing (see Box 1.2). When there is an emerging situation or an evolving trend, REA is useful for obtaining a preliminary understanding of who is affected, what kind of response may be needed, and the best strategy for implementing sustainable and culturally-relevant interventions. For example, if there are notable increases in syphilis cases related to drug use, it may be useful to carry out a REA to learn more about what kinds of drugs are being used, where they are being used, and how to reach impacted individuals and communities with prevention information. If there is a need to tailor programs or policies to

Box 1.2

Example: Problem is developing

In the aftermath of Hurricane Katrina, New Orleans experienced a demographic shift in the Latino population, particularly single, undocumented men who work as day laborers. Researchers suspected an emerging pattern of crack cocaine use among this population but needed to gather more information to begin to formulate a response. The results of REA revealed how contextual factors such as a flourishing drug market, along with social isolation and victimization of undocumented Latino day laborers, led to initiation and increased use of crack cocaine in a group that previously had relatively low use of drugs.

Adapted from Valdez et al. 2010

adapt to new challenges, gathering data through a REA may be a necessary first step.

Third, REA is useful when we need to reach hidden or vulnerable populations (see Box 1.3). REAs allow for and encourage the involvement of local community members in all aspects of the study process. Some populations may be particularly closed off and hard to reach, unless they are approached by someone known and trusted within that community. Most communities and subcultures have "gatekeepers," individuals who play a role in facilitating engagement with members of the community who may otherwise be reluctant to come forward or be interviewed. REAs often attempt to identify gatekeepers early in the process and engage them and other trusted community members to participate in the assessment.

Box 1.3

Example: Reach hidden or vulnerable populations

In December 2008, nine Senegalese men who have sex with men (MSM) were arrested and imprisoned for "acts against nature." Soon after, HIV service providers noticed a sharp decline in the use of HIV-related services among MSM. A REA was conducted to assess and document the impact of these arrests on HIV prevention efforts. A trusted network of community-based organizations was instrumental in identifying an initial pool of MSM participants to be interviewed. These MSM participants then used their personal social networks to recruit other MSM. The REA results provided documentation that increasing stigma and fear of violence associated with the 2008 arrests seriously disrupted the provision and uptake of HIV services to MSM throughout Senegal.

Adapted from Poteat et al. 2011

Box 1.4

Example: Plan or adjust a program, plan, or policy

REA was used to identify recommended practices for computerized clinical decision support and knowledge management in ambulatory clinics and community hospitals in the United States. The research team conducted REA at two hospitals and five clinics and identified ten areas such as workflow integration, well designed user interfaces, ongoing knowledge management, and intentional interaction among stakeholders that need attention to successfully implement computerized clinical decision support. REA team members also offered actionable recommendations based on findings by asking about and recording noteworthy practices of interviewees during the process of data collection, identifying the practices through debriefings and team analysis meetings, conducting member checking by asking for feedback from site report recipients, and discussing recommended practices with a panel of experts.

Adapted from Ash et al. 2012

Fourth, REA is useful when we need to plan or make adjustments to a program, plan, or policy (see Box 1.4). Findings from REA can be used as formative data for new program development or to make adjustments to ongoing programs, services, plans, or policies. Programs going through reorganization of services may benefit from assessment to identify elements of the system that are working well, along with problems in service delivery or staffing that still need to be addressed. HIV/STD prevention programs often use rapid assessment methods to adjust the hours and locations of mobile and field-based services to better reach populations in need, such as sex workers, persons who use drugs, and homeless men. Likewise, an institution or an organization may have a new plan or project they would like to carry out but may need more input from constituents or stakeholders to tailor the work. For instance, a team of anthropology students carried out a rapid assessment to understand the use of the campus' main green space to aid in the redesign of the space.

Finally, REA is useful when we need to involve the community (see Box 1.5). Often, understanding how to address a problem necessitates engagement with local community members. Having community members involved from the beginning of the research process can create support for the assessment as well as investment in the outcomes. How "community member" is defined depends upon the assessment objectives, but involving people who are directly affected by the problem means that data are likely to be more useful and result in more practical, and often achievable, recommendations. Community participation occurs at various levels. For example, community members and stakeholders can be involved in developing the plan for the assessment and helping to focus the questions and scope of the assessment. Community members are nearly always included as interview participants,

---

Box 1.5
———

Example: When community needs to be involved

In 1998, public health experts wanted to explore why, despite overall downward trends, 65% of new AIDS cases were among Black and Hispanic adults. Planners needed information on the behavioral and social context in which HIV risk behaviors occurred and how to improve strategies for reaching vulnerable individuals. Racial and ethnic minority community members in three cities helped to design, plan, and carry out a REA. Mapping and interviews carried out by local community members helped to identify patterns in the days, times, and locations that risk behaviors, such as trading sex for drugs, took place, and enabled programs to better structure service hours and outreach efforts.

Adapted from Needle et al. 2003

---

and may act as key informants, cultural "experts," or "insiders" who have a particular perspective on a problem and can offer insight into processes and structures that may not be readily apparent to outsiders. As mentioned above, community members may act as gatekeepers, but may also become full-fledged members of the data collection, analysis, and writing team, participating in all phases of the assessment and helping to formulate recommendations.

REA can be an end in itself or used as a tool that can enhance further investigations into a problem (see Box 1.6). Data collected through a rapid assessment also can contribute to the design of quantitative data collection strategies by defining important local terminology, identifying populations who may be at risk, and delineating the range of practices that may be contributing to emerging or existing challenges.

When are REAs not appropriate?

If specific quantitative information is needed—for instance, the degree or magnitude of a problem—then REA is generally not the best approach. REA is not appropriate when population-level analyses are needed. Qualitative

---

Box 1.6
———

When is REA useful?

- When we need more information about a problem.
- When the problem may be emerging or evolving.
- When we need to reach hidden or vulnerable populations.
- When we need to plan or adjust a program or policy.
- When we need to involve the community.

---

methods used in REA necessarily rely on small purposive samples that are designed to elicit deep insights and rich descriptive information. These methods are not meant to produce statistical results. However, the information and lessons learned from REAs are often broadly applicable to other programs, places, or populations. In addition, first-person narratives and examples obtained through rapid assessment can be powerful tools, either on their own or used in conjunction with quantitative results, for illustrating a problem or persuading policymakers to act.

Other factors, such as time, resources, and available expertise in qualitative methods and analysis, should also be weighed when considering whether a rapid assessment is the best approach. Following chapters cover some of these factors in more detail.

Organization of the book

In this book we provide a practical guide to REA, based on our own experience designing, implementing, and teaching REA in various contexts. We take a stepwise approach through REA, starting with the basic premise and theoretical underpinning of REA to planning and conducting research, analyzing results, and disseminating findings. Our objective is to show that REA is a fundamentally participatory, action-oriented, and community-driven approach to research that allows mutual cooperation between experts and "non-experts" in problem solving. Given our increasingly shifting social and political environment, REA may help researchers and communities to quickly act on the most pressing challenges affecting communities today. In the book, we share what we have learned with others who are interested in or committed to engaging with communities as they develop programs and policies that respond to contemporary challenges.

In the chapters that follow, we build on the REA process. Each chapter includes key points, examples, a summary, and additional resources.

In Chapter 2, "Key considerations in planning for a rapid ethnographic assessment," we introduce the reader to key concepts underlying REAs and considerations in undertaking them. We consider decisions related to the design and scope of the REA, such as the kind of expertise needed, required time and resources, and considerations in disseminating findings and results. We discuss identifying the roles of stakeholders and community members in the planning processes, along with the role of funding and funders as it relates to data ownership and publications. This is particularly important as it may have serious implications for data ownership, retention, and access. We also offer sample budget items, along with prerequisites for undertaking REA. In addition, we discuss ethical considerations within the planning process such as obtaining necessary permissions and issues related to accountability and responsibility to participants, collaborators, and the public.

In Chapter 3, "Rapid ethnographic assessment design and methods," we cover the fundamental steps in conducting REAs. We focus on fine-tuning key aims, objectives, and research questions developed during the planning phase. We describe and discuss developing sampling frames and key REA methods including ethnographic observation, ethnographic and geospatial mapping, in-depth key informant interviews, focus groups, and brief surveys. We illustrate the advantages and challenges of certain methods and explain how to make decisions about combining methods depending on the scale and scope of the research. We also include a discussion of field notes, and how to ensure that team members know how to appropriately record their notes. Finally, we discuss the pros and cons of recording and transcribing interviews versus relying on notes.

In Chapter 4, "Fieldwork," we focus on the fundamentals of team-based fieldwork. We offer advice about how to put together a research team—specifically, who should be on the team and how the team should be organized. We also discuss considerations for including community members who may not be trained researchers. We pay special attention to the issue of skills transfer and the potential for building research and assessment capacity in communities where research is not the norm. We also cover team debriefings, their purpose, and how to make them productive. We discuss field safety in general, along with practical considerations for understanding issues related to gendered, racial, ethnic, and power dynamics of fieldwork. Finally, we discuss fieldwork ethics, including research values, informed consent, and confidentiality, along with common ethical dilemmas and conflicts which arise in team-based, community-driven participatory research.

In Chapter 5, "Data analysis," we provide an in-depth overview and practical step-by-step instruction on qualitative data management, qualitative data analysis, and triangulation. We specifically detail practical and logistical issues related to rapid data analysis including the construction of the aims and objectives of analysis, analytical styles, data preparation and management in team-based research, issues of reliability and validity, and computer-based qualitative analysis software. In addition, we offer practical advice about how to compose and manage an effective analytical team, and considerations for including and engaging community members in analysis.

In Chapter 6, "Report writing and follow up," we offer guidance on how to construct and present key findings and outcomes based on audience, but especially to decision makers, program administrators, and policy makers. We provide specific instruction for writing clear and concrete recommendations for a variety of audiences, developing a dissemination plan for findings, and creating a follow-up plan for addressing further needs. Finally, we discuss the potential challenges and solutions related to community-engaged work that may arise during the analytical and dissemination phases.

In Chapter 7, "Case studies," we provide rich comprehensive information on three case studies. These case studies serve to illustrate the range, size, and scope of REAs, including small and large REAs and US and internationally-based REAs, reflecting both jurisdictional as well as cross-cultural parameters related to scale that need critical consideration.

In the final section, "Additional Resources and Appendices," we include additional materials and information that we consider to be essential, including a glossary of terms, sample budget, and project planning tool, and additional resources such as web-links and references. We designed this chapter to serve as the basis for materials to be included in a companion website for students and instructors.

Finally, our key objective throughout the book is to provide a useful guide to students, researchers, and practitioners interested in conducting applied qualitative research, assessment, or evaluation in public health, education, cultural resource management, and other fields. We feel strongly that REAs are increasingly relevant for governments, non-governmental institutions and organizations, researchers, and communities in an ever-changing social and political landscape.

Box 1.7

Summary

- REA is a qualitative research method that focuses on the collection and analysis of locally relevant data and is used to quickly assess a variety of complex social and structural issues in order to improve programs and policies impacting marginalized and vulnerable populations.
- REA is an equity-driven approach to research, one that includes communities in the collaboration of both the acquisition of knowledge and its utilization.
- REA has deep roots in international health and development and draws on principles of ethnography and anthropological sensibility.
- REA is appropriate to use in contexts where we need information about a problem that is emerging or evolving, when we need to reach hidden or vulnerable populations, when we need to plan or make changes to programs or policies, or when we to involve the community.
- REA is not appropriate in situations where specific quantitative information or population-level analyses are needed.

References

Ash, Joan S., Dean F. Sittig, Kenneth P. Guappone, Richard H. Dykstra, Joshua Richardson, Adam Wright, James Carpenter et al. 2012. Recommended practices for computerized clinical decision support and knowledge management in community settings: a qualitative study. *BMC Medical Informatics and Decision Making* 12(1): 6.

Baba, Marietta L. 2000. Theories of practice in anthropology: A critical appraisal. *NAPA Bulletin* 18(1):17–44.

Beebe, James. 2001. *Rapid Assessment Process: An Introduction.* Walnut Creek, CA: AltaMira Press.

Beebe, James. 2014. *Rapid Qualitative Inquiry: A Field Guide to Team-Based Assessment.* Lanham, MD: Rowman & Littlefield.

Bejarano, Carolina A., Lucia López Juárez, Mirian A. Mijangos García, and Daniel M. Goldstein. 2019. *Decolonizing Ethnography: Undocumented Immigrants and New Directions in Social Science*. Durham, NC: Duke University Press.

Burks, Derek J., Rockey Robbins, and Jayson P. Durtschi. 2011. American Indian gay, bisexual and two-spirit men: a rapid assessment of HIV/AIDS risk factors, barriers to prevention and culturally-sensitive intervention. *Culture, Health & Sexuality* 13(3): 283–298.

Chambers, Erve. 1979. The burden of profession: Applied anthropology at the crossroads. *Reviews in Anthropology* 6(4): 523–540.

Chambers, Robert. 1994. The origins and practice of participatory rural appraisal. *World Development* 22(7): 953–969.

Fals Borda, Orlando. 2001. "Participatory (action) research in social theory: Origins and challenges." In *Handbook of Action Research: Participative Inquiry and Practice*, edited by Hilary Bradbury and Peter Reason, 27–37. Thousand Oaks, CA: Sage Publications.

Fitch Chris and Gerry V. Stimson. 2003. *RAR Review: An International Mapping and Retrospective Evaluation Study of Rapid Assessments Conducted on Drug Use*. Geneva, Switzerland: World Health Organization.

Freire, Paulo. 2006. *Pedagogy of the Oppressed*, 30th Anniversary ed. New York, NY: Continuum.

Galtung, Johan. 1967. *Theory and Methods of Social Research*. New York, NY: Columbia University Press.

Greenhalgh, Trisha, Ellen Annandale, Richard Ashcroft, James Barlow, Nick Black, Alan Bleakley, Ruth Boaden et al. 2016. An open letter to The BMJ editors on qualitative research. *British Medical Journal* 352: i563.

Gupta, Akhil and James Ferguson, eds. 1997. *Anthropological Locations: Boundaries and Grounds of a Field Science*. Berkeley, CA: University of California Press.

Harrison, Faye, ed. 1997. *Decolonizing Anthropology: Moving Further Toward an Anthropology for Liberation*. Arlington, VA: American Anthropological Association.

Hymes, Dell, ed. 1969. *Reinventing Anthropology*. New York, NY: Pantheon Books.

Israel, Barbara A., Chris M. Coombe, Rebecca R. Cheezum, Amy J. Schulz, Robert J. McGranaghan, Richard Lichtenstein, Angela G. Reyes, Jaye Clement, and Akosua Burris. 2010. Community-based participatory research: a capacity-building approach for policy advocacy aimed at eliminating health disparities. *American Journal of Public Health* 100(11): 2094–2102.

LeCompte, Margaret D. 2002. The transformation of ethnographic practices: Past and current challenges. *Qualitative Research* 2(3): 283–299.

Manderson, Lenore. 1996. *Population and Reproductive Health Programmes: Applying Rapid Anthropological Assessment Procedures*. New York, NY: United Nations Population Fund.

Minkler, Meredith and Nina Wallerstein, eds. 2011. *Community-Based Participatory Research for Health: From Process to Outcomes*. San Francisco, CA: John Wiley & Sons.

Nader, Laura. 1969. "Up the anthropologist—perspectives gained from studying up." In *Reinventing Anthropology*, edited by Dell Hymes, 284–311. New York, NY: Pantheon Books.

Needle, Richard H., Robert T. Trotter, Merrill Singer, Christopher Bates, J. Bryan Page, David Metzger, and Louis H. Marcelin. 2003. Rapid assessment of the HIV/AIDS crisis in racial and ethnic minority communities: an approach for timely community interventions. *American Journal of Public Health* 93(6): 970–979.

Parker III, Theodore A., and Brent Bailey, eds. 1991. *A biological assessment of the Alto Madidi region and adjacent areas of Northwest Bolivia*. Washington DC: Conservation International Rapid Assessment Program.

Poteat, Tonia, Daouda Diouf, Fatou Maria Drame, Marieme Ndaw, Cheikh Traore, Mandeep Dhaliwal, Chris Beyrer, and Stefan Baral. 2011. HIV risk among MSM in Senegal: a qualitative rapid assessment of the impact of enforcing laws that criminalize same sex practices. *PloS ONE* 6(12): e28760.

Reiter, Bernd and Ulrich Oslender, eds. 2014. *Bridging Scholarship and Activism Reflections from the Frontlines of Collaborative Research*. East Lansing, MI: Michigan State University Press.

Schatz, Edward, ed. 2009. *Political Ethnography: What Immersion Contributes to the Study of Power*. Chicago, IL: University of Chicago Press.

Scrimshaw, Nevin S., and Gary R. Gleason, eds. 1992. *Rapid Assessment Procedures: Qualitative Methodologies for Planning and Evaluation of Health Related Programmes*. Boston: International Nutrition Foundation for Developing Countries.

Smith, Linda T. 2012. *Decolonizing Methodologies: Research and Indigenous Peoples*. London and New York: Zed Books Ltd.

Spradley, James P. 1980. *Participant Observation*. Belmont, CA: Wadsworth.

Trotter, Robert T., Richard H. Needle, Eric Goosby, Christopher Bates, and Merrill Singer. 2001. A methodological model for rapid assessment, response, and evaluation: the RARE program in public health. *Field Methods* 13(2): 137–159.

Trouillot, Michel-Rolph. 2003. *Global Transformations: Anthropology and the Modern World*. New York: Palgrave Macmillan.

Valdez, Avelardo, Alice Cepeda, Nalini Junko Negi, and Charles Kaplan. 2010. Fumando la piedra: Emerging patterns of crack use among Latino immigrant day laborers in New Orleans. *Journal of Immigrant and Minority Health* 12(5): 737–742.

2 Key considerations in planning for a rapid ethnographic assessment

Key learning outcomes

1 Identify the types of questions REA can best address
2 Generate focused assessment questions
3 Understand time and resources needed
4 Recognize best practices for disseminating findings
5 Decide on stakeholder roles and research design
6 Anticipate funding guidelines and terms

Whether the REA results in useful and actionable findings depends a great deal on how well planned and implemented the REA is. Devoting considerable time and thought to the planning stages of a research study can make all the difference to the integrity of your work. Planning presents a valuable opportunity for the REA team to generate ideas, conduct literature reviews, decide on the focus of research, choose appropriate methodological tools, determine site locations and groups with whom to work, prepare a timeline and budget, and conduct preliminary site visits and interviews. Careful planning and organization, therefore, leads to better preparation for fieldwork, data collection, and analysis.

In this chapter, we discuss basic considerations and questions that need to be addressed at the very early stages of considering a REA. We go over the kinds of research questions that REAs are best designed to address, and whether REA is appropriate for certain types of research or programmatic questions. We consider decisions related to the design and scope of the REA and the lay and technical expertise that may be needed to carry out a project. We will also review resources such as staffing, time, and funding. Not least, we will discuss the need to determine the audience for the REA and the roles of funders, stakeholders, and community members in shaping the direction and scope of the REA. Finally, we will explore issues of data ownership and retention.

What to consider before planning the REA

An organization, community, or set of stakeholders often undertakes a REA because it needs more information about a problem, and conducting a REA can be a fast, easy, and relatively inexpensive way to learn more. But first, the REA practitioner—the person with technical expertise or experience in conducting REA—needs to help those who wish to undertake a REA determine which research questions are most important to them, and whether those questions can be answered through REA. To a novice, REAs may look deceptively easy to execute. As some on our REA teams initially have mistakenly observed, "You're just talking to people—how hard can that be?" Moreover, one criticism of REAs is that, if not well executed, they elicit nothing new or gain no new knowledge. The planning process will help determine whether REA is likely to be a good fit for the program.

REA can certainly be used for the purposes of documentation: for instance, to gather stakeholders' views on a well-understood problem that can later be galvanized into policy action. However, in most cases, program managers or researchers are looking to the REA to do more. They want the REA to help explain or provide new insight into a problem or situation. In other words, they want the REA to supplement what is already known and to provide additional evidence that can be used to improve services or a particular situation. Therefore, it is important to lay a foundation of understanding about the overall project—the key research questions, the benefits and challenges of using REA, and what expertise and resources may be needed—before diving into planning for the REA (see Box 2.1).

First, it is important to ask a few fundamental, overarching questions to determine whether REA is the best fit for the problem. Early on, it is important to have a discussion of the kinds of issues or questions that researchers or partner organizations would like the REA to explore or answer. There are often competing interests and goals that drive interest in REA, and it is important to be realistic about what the REA is likely to achieve. Ask the stakeholders or funders to articulate an answer to the question: If the REA could answer one or two research or programmatic questions, what would those questions be? What do funders want to accomplish given the time and resources? This is important because the scope of most REAs needs to be narrow rather than broad, allowing data collection to focus thoroughly on a few key areas or topics. REAs that try to cover too much ground tend to result in "thin" rather than "rich" data.

Data obtained during the REA is garnered through a core set of qualitative methods: namely in-depth interviewing, ethnographic mapping, direct and participant observation, and sometimes brief surveys. An interdisciplinary team carries out data collection, which strengthens the quality of the data and the subsequent analysis. These aspects of fieldwork and data collection will be discussed in later chapters. REA methods, which are designed to elicit insight and description rather than to measure frequency or magnitude, are based on small samples designed for depth, rather than breadth.

In many settings, REA practitioners may find themselves interacting with professionals who are much more familiar with other types of research based on quantitative and survey methods—methods that rely on large samples and

Box 2.1

Overview of planning considerations

- Is this the right approach for the assessment questions?

  o   What will be added by using this approach?
  o   Will findings based on qualitative data be persuasive?

- What is the timeline for using the data?

  o   When does the program need to use the findings?

- Who else needs to be involved (in planning, data collection, analysis, approvals)?

  o   Who are the essential people?
  o   What role will they have?
  o   How will stakeholders be involved?

- Who should be interviewed and why?
- What locations might the team need to observe or conduct fieldwork?
- What methods should the team use and why?
- What kind of skills and expertise will be needed?

  o   Topical expertise
  o   Cultural proficiency
  o   Ability to adapt to changes in the field
  o   Ability to work in teams
  o   Interviewing skills
  o   Training in qualitative methods/analysis

- How will the data be managed and handled?

  o   Recording, transcribing, translating

- How big should the REA be?

  o   What is the scope and scale of the project?

- What resources are needed and available to carry out the project?
- What approvals are necessary and how long will it take to get them?

findings based on statistical probabilities. REAs can be effective for explaining or describing things about process, motivations, perceptions, and other similar areas. But they are not appropriate for answering questions about the magnitude and frequency of a problem. Therefore, questions about population size, disease prevalence, or demographic changes may not be a good match for a REA. For instance, when a state health department wanted to know more about the STD prevention needs of Latino migrant men, the REA was able to gather data about how men made contact with sex workers, about the organization of female sex work in the area, and about the living conditions and work environments of migrant workers. This descriptive data helped the state and its partners better understand the context in which STD risk took place, which informed strategies for reaching migrant men and sex workers. The REA was not meant to measure the size of these populations, however, or to formally assess the prevalence of STDs in them.

After identifying the key research questions, practitioners should reflect on how the REA will complement what is already known about the problem, and what it will add to the existing knowledge base. As with all projects in general, it is essential to do preliminary or background work to determine what the existing evidence is, if any. Conduct a review of the published literature. Are there other surveys or studies that have been conducted or are underway that might shed light on the topic? A desk review of other materials may include data sources such as surveillance and program monitoring data, as well as internal reports and other "gray" literature. Often a search of the gray literature through online internet searches or through networks of contacts will yield earlier work related to the topic such as unpublished internal reports, needs or situation assessment reports, meeting summaries, and presentations. Review these materials and then ask: What are the strengths in existing data? Where are the gaps in data? Can a REA help fill these gaps (see Box 2.2)?

In addition to the literature search, taking the time to speak with key stakeholders in the early stages of a project will help the team gain a better understanding of the work that has already been done and obtain contextual information. In advance of the REA mentioned above, the team contacted individuals in local community-based organizations and academic institutions by phone to inform them about the impending REA and obtain their advice and opinions about various topics related to the population. These calls were not formal interviews, but they were incredibly helpful in terms of identifying potential key informants and enabling the team to better understand the local health care context. If time and funding allow, a preliminary site visit, along with meetings and discussions with stakeholders, should be done as part of the process of planning. This type of evaluative assessment

---

Box 2.2

What to consider before planning REA

- If the REA could answer one or two questions, what would those questions be? What do we want to accomplish given our time and resources?
- What is already known about the problem or issue? What are the strengths in existing data? What are the gaps in data? Can a REA help fill these gaps?
- Are the goals for the REA reasonable?

might shed light on the kinds of methods to use, who to interview, which sites to visit, and potential ethical conflicts.

Planners also need to consider how the REA findings will be used. While studies and surveys often add to the body of knowledge about a topic, the primary goal of REA is to gather data that can be used for practical purposes. Urging planners and stakeholders to articulate how the data will be used and for what purposes will help the REA team focus on what is most pressing and important for them to learn about and to consider what may actually be achievable through a REA.

Once planners have considered key research questions, background information, and how findings will be used, drafting a concept proposal outlining the REA can prove useful in guiding discussions with potential partners and funders. A concept proposal is brief and succinct (e.g., one to three pages) and usually includes the purpose, description, and objectives of the REA, the methods to be used, and how analysis will be conducted.

What kind of technical expertise will be needed?

Ideally, REAs will be led by or have team members with training in ethnographic and/or qualitative methods. Training in the social sciences, ethnography, or in participatory qualitative methods specifically can help ensure the REA results in high-quality, meaningful data. For instance, high-quality data begins with carefully constructed interview questions and guides that gently lead interviewees through a focused "conversation" about a topic. It requires well-trained interviewers with strong listening skills who can establish rapport with a participant and keep the interview on track without making the participant feel rushed by the process or led by the interview questions.

Depending on time and resources, REAs may include a variety of data collectors and analysts, some of whom may not have had experience conducting research or been trained in qualitative methods. Smaller REAs, for instance, may include staff who take part in REAs for the experience as part of or in addition to their regular duties at partner organizations. Bigger projects with more resources may include funds to hire interviewers to carry out a project. Regardless of who makes up the REA team, someone on the project needs to be qualified to train data collectors in the methods being used, including interviewing skills such as elicitation techniques, focused listening, structured observation, and note taking. Individuals with these skills may be found at local universities or in organizations that have previously conducted REAs. This will lead to better data: poorly conducted assessments often lead to results that are obvious and predictable.

Another kind of technical expertise that will be needed is cultural proficiency. Cultural proficiency refers to the knowledge and expertise that someone may have about the problem, the community, or the population that is the focus of the REA. In anthropology, cultural experts are traditionally referred to as "insiders"—people who have direct experience with the

---

Box 2.3

What kind of expertise is needed to carry out the REA?

- How will the data collection take place? Who should lead the data collection?
- How will the analysis be handled? Who will lead the analysis?
- How will community members be included in the process of data collection and analysis?
- Who has the ethnographic expertise available to help guide the REA?

---

problem and who may have insight into why certain things are occurring. Cultural experts may also be privy to information and contacts that the REA team needs. They may function as gatekeepers, individuals with access to knowledgeable community members who may be otherwise hard for the REA team to identify or reach.

In addition to ethnographic and cultural expertise, the REA will need topical expertise; that is, individuals with knowledge of or experience with the topic under investigation (see Box 2.3). Topical expertise helps inform planning, framing of research questions, and protocol development. Topical experts also participate in fieldwork. We will discuss the REA team in more detail in a later chapter.

Additionally, when planning the REA, the team should decide how to handle the analysis. Should an ethnographer lead the analysis? Ideally, the person leading the analysis is part of the REA team and has been involved in field work and data collection, rather than someone entirely new to the project. In the best examples, the team includes local community members in both the data collection and analysis, thus transferring research skills to the community.

REAs generate large amounts of qualitative data, and most projects benefit from the use of software programs that help manage and reduce qualitative data for the purposes of analysis; having someone trained to use such a program is essential. A common misperception is that qualitative data analysis programs "do" analysis—they do not. Analysis requires someone to read each interview, think about the data, and develop and refine coding schemes in a systematic approach that ensures the integrity of the findings. Software programs help analysts manage, categorize, and sort the large volume of qualitative data produced during a REA and speed up the process. More detailed discussion of methods and analysis is included in later chapters.

What kind of time and resources will be needed?

Considerations related to timeline for the data are critical to discuss during the REA planning phase (see Box 2.4). When are the findings needed? Is the timeline achievable? Again, the emphasis on usable data is key here.

Box 2.4

What kind of time and resources are needed?

*   When are the findings needed?
*   Can the timeline be achieved? Is it possible to carry out the REA, analyze the data, and produce a report of findings within the time allotted?
*   How much time is needed to secure the necessary approvals?
*   How much funding is needed? Who will fund it? Are the necessary human, technical, and financial resources available?

If the data are needed to inform policymakers, is it possible to carry out the REA, analyze the data, and produce a report of findings within the time allotted? Often, data may be needed to inform a designated planning period or budget deadline. If the timeline is not feasible, then perhaps another method is more appropriate.

A common question is: how long will the REA take? The answer is, it depends on the size and scope of the REA, the funding, and how quickly data can be collected. REAs can be focused on an individual site or community with a relatively small number of interviews or can be developed as larger, multi-site projects. It is important to remember that REAs are meant to be carried out quickly so that data and findings are current and timely and can be used for action. Although there is no set rule about how long is long enough for a REA, most experts agree that the time spent in the field collecting data for a REA should probably be between two and six weeks.

Some REAs are necessarily time-limited due to funding, travel restrictions, and the need to limit disruption of program operations, staff routines, and community activities. Most state health departments, for example, do not have the budget or staff to spend months carrying out a REA. In our work, we were involved with REAs that took as little as a week to collect data, as well as large, complex REAs in which data collection took place in multiple sites in several cities. These larger projects took several weeks or even months to complete data collection. Once the REA team determines the purpose of the REA and agrees on the set of questions it should answer, they can then decide on the types or categories of participants to interview (e.g., clients, providers, policy makers) and sites for conducting fieldwork. The scale and scope of a REA is dependent on many variables, including issues of access, time, and available resources.

As in all research endeavors, there is a need to balance scope with the feasibility of providing results in a timely manner. How much time will you need to prepare, train staff, collect the data, and then conduct analysis? Are the technical and electronic resources readily available or will you need to procure personnel, materials, and software? In low resourced sites, it may be necessary to allow more time for logistics, transport, or training. Staff literacy

	April	May	June	July	Aug	Sept
Planning	■					
Protocol & Approvals		■				
Training		■				
Data Collection			■			
Data Cleaning & Analysis				■	■	
Report Writing & Dissemination					■	■

Figure 2.1 Sample timeline.

may be an issue in some settings, or the infrastructure may not support electronic data transfer. All of these aspects should be considered before enlarging the scope and scale of the REA, and care taken to ensure that results can be delivered in a timely manner. In collecting qualitative data, the goal is to collect a relatively small number of high-quality interviews; how much data are needed depends upon the quality of interviews and the concept of saturation, the point at which nothing new is being learned. This concept is covered in more detail in the next two chapters. The desire to expand the scope, or add more sites and more interviews, must always be weighed against the additional burden and cost in terms of time and human and financial resources.

REA practitioners also need to add in time for protocol development and review, including Institutional Review Board (IRB) approval if necessary. Projects funded by the US government may require approval from the Office of Management and Budget (OMB). As part of planning, inquire as to what approvals are necessary and how long the process of approval may take. Depending upon the project and the funding agency, some review and approval processes can be quite lengthy. Determine early on how much time these are likely to take and build this into the timeline. We suggest using visual tools such as a table or Gantt chart to lay out tasks (see Figure 2.1). It is important to be realistic about how long various stages will take so that the work is not rushed, or worse, unable to be completed.

Who is the audience for the assessment and how will the findings be disseminated?

One of the most important questions to ask in the early stages of planning is who is the audience for the assessment—who is the REA report meant to inform? Is it meant to be an internal program document or do funders plan to share the findings more broadly, with other stakeholders and community members? Although plans may change, having this discussion early on helps clarify expectations and may generate useful ideas about how to best disseminate the findings. Most REAs result in a written report or summary of findings, but there may also be products such as presentations at community forums and scientific conferences and published manuscripts. Clarify which products are to be prioritized and what the role of the team will be in producing them. We will cover report writing in more detail in a later chapter.

What role do the stakeholders have?

Stakeholders are generally defined as persons in the local group who are likely to be affected by the REA findings or any subsequent activities that result from it (Beebe 2001). These can include users as well as providers of services, along with persons responsible for governance; for example, staff in state and local health departments, representatives from community-based organizations and social service agencies, and members of the target population.

A REA can be a catalyst for raising awareness and taking action on issues that affect communities. Successful REAs are collaborations in which community members who are not traditional or trained researchers work together with the REA team to carry out the assessment and plan for follow-up activities. Community members help determine priorities for the assessment and are frequently involved in data collection and analysis. In this way, REAs not only harness local knowledge about a problem and possible solutions but also help build capacity in communities to conduct research and implement interventions. They represent an opportunity for local organizations to work together, fostering or strengthening local partnerships. Involving community members and other stakeholders from the start can help create a positive environment, generating support for the work to be done and investment in the outcomes.

Depending on the scope and objectives of the REA, stakeholders may have different roles or levels of involvement. Stakeholders may be involved in an advisory capacity, helping with the early stages of planning and focusing the REA, or they may have a larger role in conducting the REA. Some stakeholders may be involved in data collection, although it is important to emphasize that stakeholders must undergo training and adhere to the principles and guidelines of the project if they plan to be involved. Choosing who and at what phase they will be involved takes careful consideration. For instance, it is generally not good practice, and may be unethical, to have stakeholders observing or witnessing interviews due to issues of confidentiality. In our REAs, we often had staff and managers ask to "sit in" on interviews, but we usually refused, explaining how this can interfere with rapport and violate confidentiality protections. There also may be power dynamics that can affect the REA, especially when stakeholders who are in positions of power are involved. In one REA, conducted in a small city, we trained health department staff to conduct interviews. We did not anticipate that, in some instances, frontline staff would end up interviewing upper management about budget issues. This power differential was a source of discomfort and stress for both staff and managers and likely led to guarded responses and a lack of rapport in some interviews. These aspects should be considered before engaging individual stakeholders in direct data collection.

On the other hand, we strongly recommend engaging community stake-holders from the beginning as active participants and collaborators. We encourage recruiting members of the target population as members of the REA team whenever possible. Community outreach workers and lay health workers, for example, have made excellent interviewers and contributed sub-stantially to projects because of their knowledge of the target population and local context and their personal investment in the project outcomes. This ensures that the REA reflects community-driven goals and facilitates self-determination and shared control of the research process by members of targeted communities. REAs are most successful when they are guided by a diverse team of people who are invested in mitigating the problem and who represent a variety of perspectives.

In our experience, working with a small stakeholder group that can be involved for the duration of the project—setting priorities, collecting and analyzing data, and disseminating findings—is preferable to working with a large, disparate group of stakeholders. Large groups can be challenging to manage, less cohesive, and have individuals with competing interests or who tend to drift in and out with little interest in the project. A small group of stakeholders that is invested in the success of the REA can be engaged in making decisions at key junctures and be given regular updates. Their input may be invaluable as the project progresses because they often come from the community in which the REA is taking place and have close rela-tionships with and may be members of the target population. However, it may be necessary or advantageous to hold meetings with a broader group of stakeholders to solicit input before planning begins, to share findings, and discuss action plans based on outcomes. In any case, defining and discuss-ing the objectives and the basic design and scope of the project (e.g., sites, number of interviews, who will be interviewed) can help the REA team and stakeholders come to an agreement about the overall shape and substance of the project.

How much funding is needed?

REAs are relatively inexpensive compared to large studies, but they still con-sume valuable and often scarce resources. REA teams are accountable to funders and sponsoring agencies for managing resources well and ethically. The cost of REAs can vary dramatically—as government anthropologists, we worked on REAs that ranged in cost from a few thousand dollars to

---

Box 2.5

Sample budget considerations

- Salary/Consultant Fees/Staffing costs (e.g., interviewers, administrative help)
- Institutional overhead (i.e., indirect costs)
- Travel and accommodation costs (e.g., air fare, hotel, car rental, per diem)
- Equipment and software
- Participant incentives or tokens of appreciation for interview participants
- Transcription and translation costs
- Printing costs
- Phone/internet services
- Rental costs for meeting or interviewing space

---

hundreds of thousands of dollars, depending on the scale and scope of the project. No matter what the cost of the project, discussions of the budget and available resources are an integral part of planning the project.

Most REAs will require a detailed budget prior to starting the project. In addition to travel costs, there will be costs for staffing, training, transcription, tokens of appreciation, the cost of software programs to be used in the analysis, and costs associated with producing a report (see Box 2.5). Add to these potential costs for equipment (e.g., digital recorders or laptops) and rental costs for interviewing or office space, if needed. If the REA is contracted out to a research organization, there will also be overhead costs in addition to these expenses.

Dividing the project into phases—protocol development, staffing, training, fieldwork, analysis/report writing, dissemination—or similar meaningful chunks is a good way to think concretely about the various tasks involved and what they will cost. For example, what costs if any will be associated with protocol development and approvals? How many interviewers will be needed and what will they be paid? How many laptops or digital recorders will be needed? Is there enough money in the budget to transcribe interviews? Although things may change, entering these items and costs into a table or spreadsheet is a necessary part of the process and a means of tracking what has been done. It also helps keep goals realistic and in line with resources. Some researchers have had the disappointing and wasteful experience of expending large amounts of effort to collect data, only to learn that the project has no money left for the analysis.

Some large REAs may also need statements of work (SOW) or position descriptions to be written for parts of the project. For example, if a large REA is seeking to hire interviewers, the SOW will include a description of the work to be done, the skill set needed, the amount of time needed to carry out the work, and hourly rates. The SOW becomes part of the budget proposal and provides justification for funding requests. A SOW may also be required by partner organizations when their staff work on the REA. The SOW serves as a way to document the organization's contribution in terms of time and (human and material) resources.

All REAs require financial support, even if they are led by students or staff as part of their regular work duties or educational training. There are multiple sources of funding: self-funding, internal funding from one's own institution, collaborating with those who have funding resources available, and applying for grants from research bodies or specialized institutions that would be interested in the area of study. At times, proposals for funding can be successful at the onset of research; other times, funding may be possible or could emerge for later stages of the REA. Critical to requesting funds is preparing a preliminary budget which may require some adjustment once the research process sets in. In addition, REA practitioners often work with community members or other stakeholders who may need to be monetarily compensated for their time because participation in the REA would amount to loss of working hours and wages.

Who has control of the data and to whom are REA practitioners accountable?

Finally, addressing issues of data "ownership" or control of the data is a crucial part of the planning process and often a matter of negotiation, while at the same time subject to rules that govern some types of funding. It is often mistakenly assumed that those who conduct research own or control the use of the resulting data. However, funders, employers, research organizations, and research participants may impose conditions that dictate otherwise. Funders, because they provide financial support for different reasons, may require that data be used and disseminated in a particular way. Rules that apply to federal government funds, for instance, stipulate that researchers be given the right to use data collected with public funds for the public good (Steneck 2007). However, researchers may be obliged to share the data as a benefit to society and to bolster impact of data.

It is also important to distinguish between grants and contracts when a project receives government funding. Under rules that apply to federal grants, funding provided to researchers and institutions is meant to assist them in carrying out the research and gives the researcher substantial control over the project and the data (US Department of Health and Human Services 2018). Contracts, on the other hand, are used by the federal government to procure a product or service; the resulting product is usually owned and controlled by the government. The difference between contracts and grants are significant and determines who has the right to disseminate and publish the results and findings of the REA.

Research, non-profit organizations, or for-profit institutions, on the other hand, often retain or release data ownership rights depending on their interests. These institutions are often responsible for budgets, regulatory

---

Box 2.6

Data ownership and accountability considerations

- Who owns the data collected during the REA?
- What are my obligations in collecting these data?
- What rights do I have to disseminate or publish the data?

---

compliance, contractual obligations, and data management. As a result, they may have rights and obligations to retain control over the data collected with funds given to them. Further, research participants or community groups that serve as sources of data increasingly claim or seek some control over research results.

Very early in the planning process, it is important to consider how and what kinds of data will be disseminated and shared and the relations, agreements, and, sometimes, the regulations that may govern these processes (see Box 2.6). There are both ethical and practical considerations to data dissemination and sharing. For instance, data may put some participants in danger or may be used by others in ways that were not originally intended by the REA team. Measures to remove personal identifiers, redact sensitive information, or otherwise "anonymize" data may be enough to protect against such potential harm. However, the process of anonymizing data can be imperfect, complicated, and problematic since all data have some potential to identify their source. We strongly suggest that the REA protocol contain specific information outlining (1) who is able to have access to data for the purposes of potentially reanalyzing the data or extending the original set of analyses, and (2) who is able to use the findings for dissemination (e.g., publications, presentations).

We also suggest that the protocol include how to preserve or destroy the data at the end of the project. Most IRBs will require that a protocol include language that stipulates what measures will be taken to secure, store, and destroy raw data as part of human subjects protections. In most qualitative projects, including REAs, it is common practice to destroy any interview recordings after transcription has occurred and to de-identify transcripts to protect personally identifiable information. However, additional discussion may be needed to determine whether de-identified transcripts will be destroyed after analysis has taken place, whether these will be stored for a specified period of time, and who, if anyone, may have access to these for any subsequent analysis.

In addition, as stated earlier, just because the REA team has conducted the assessment does not always mean that they have latitude to publish the findings. Again, this is a matter for negotiation and, in ideal circumstances, becomes an opportunity for collaboration among researchers, stakeholders, and the sponsoring agency or funder. Since data ownership provisions can be complex, those who undertake REAs need to be aware of their obligations before they begin collecting data. Additionally, these provisions often must be approved by the institution that receives and is ultimately responsible for the administration of funding. Therefore, REA practitioners should make sure to get institutional approval before entering into formal and informal agreements that affect the control and use of data.

Expectations regarding accountability for a REA practitioner can be very different from traditional models within academic anthropology where the IRB process has been noted by some as a bureaucratic stumbling block to conducting engaged ethnographic research (Bosk and De Vries 2004; Fluehr-Lobban 1994; Heimer and Petty 2010; Lederman 2006, 2007; Librett and Perrone 2010). In a REA, funding and fieldwork contexts can prove complex because projects are inherently collaborative and involve many different institutions and individuals who may have a wide range of ethical issues, positions, and agreements at stake. However, we would emphasize that even for anthropologists being trained in traditional academic departments, issues of accountability to research participants, collaborators, funders, and other stakeholders need to be taken into account early in the research process, at the planning stages, well beyond the considerations related to formal ethical protocols.

What are some ethical considerations during planning?

There are several ethical issues to consider during the planning of a REA. Since most REA projects seek to engage with human subjects, they must first be reviewed and approved by the appropriate IRB. Federal regulations and institutional policy require an IRB to approve any research project or assessment prior to data collection if the work engages human subjects. This measure is meant to ensure that the research will not harm individuals and communities as a result of project processes or findings. Often, as part of this process, the REA practitioner may have to include letters of support or memorandums of understanding with any participating partner institutions indicating that the REA team has been given permission to conduct the research. Partnering organizations, especially large ones, may have their own IRB process that the REA team may have to go through to obtain approval. REAs are often conducted on behalf of an institution or agency, such as a government agency, community-based organization, or hospital; these entities often have IRBs that require review and approval.

REAs represent an equity-focused approach to research. Normative practices of social sciences or health research often privilege the researcher or the institution through which the research is made possible (e.g., university, funding agencies). However, the authority of the researcher is highly debated in many qualitative research traditions, including anthropology (Smith 2005). There have been efforts to acknowledge differential power relations between researchers and participants, and some have resulted in movement towards establishing research paradigms focused on more equitable relations between the two parties (Bhattacharya 2008; Smith 2005; Visweswaran 1997). In planning for a REA, it is particularly important to recognize that these relationships, although central to guiding the approach of a REA, are often continuously negotiated throughout the research process. There may be various shifts in "inferior" or "superior" knowledge positions, and researchers and participants may have dual roles as both insiders and outsiders. At times, the researcher may be highly dependent on participants' knowledge about the phenomena under study and on their willingness to share these perspectives.

In planning for a REA, it's important to create a research context, from the very beginning, that will diminish the distance between researchers and participants and engender an anti-authoritative researcher–researched relationship. This means confronting complex negotiations about the research agenda, about which knowledge is to be counted as relevant, shifts in "inferior" and "superior" knowledge positions, as well as ethical dilemmas. Such considerations should help researchers understand that research interactions, rather than being predetermined or fixed, are tentative processes that continually shift, reflecting the changing nature of how we conceptualize the roles of others.

Why is planning crucial to the success of the REA?

In anthropology, ethnographic research often consists of an "open-ended" or "emergent" design, with the understanding that the research design, questions, and data will unfold once the researcher is in the field (Miles, Huberman, and Saldaña 2014; Punch 1994). In contrast, given the rapid, focused, and practical nature of REAs, research questions and the design should be structured as much as possible ahead of the actual data collection, with some room for flexibility during field work. Structured here means having one or two focused research questions laid out and knowing how they are connected to each other and the broader framework of the assessment; knowing what kinds of data will be collected and why, the methods to be used, and in what sequence; and knowing the structure of the data (e.g., narrative, maps) and how it will be analyzed. Having a focused set of research questions, for example, can guide initial data collection activities, saving time and resources and helping to avoid confusion and overload. Focused questions can also make it easier to communicate about the purpose of the REA to funders, stakeholders, and community participants, which can be beneficial in facilitating support and approval for the REA. Thus, there are many concrete benefits in developing draft protocols that include research questions, budget and staffing needs, training and fieldwork preparation plans, and data analysis and dissemination plans during the planning phase.

It is also important to note that not everything can be worked out in advance in qualitative research. REAs should have a set of clear research questions and design determined in advance during the planning process before data are collected. But REAs also need to be flexible to adapt to any issues that may emerge during the course of data collection. For instance, we do not recommend having pre-established categories or coding schemes before data are collected. Rather, we advocate that interpretation of data—categories, codes, and themes—emerge iteratively during collection and analysis. In summary, structure is desirable to a REA, and some amount of structure is necessary before the assessment is carried out.

Box 2.7

Summary

- Good planning is essential to the success of REA.
- Review existing data and knowledge to determine what the REA will add.
- REA requires consensus about one to two key assessment questions on which to focus.
- Successful REAs are built on a combination of ethnographic/qualitative expertise, cultural proficiency, and content (topical) expertise.
- REA results are meant to be timely; so it is crucial to determine if the timeline is achievable.
- Budgeting facilitates good stewardship of human and financial resources.
- REA is a collaborative, shared effort between the team and the community. Engage with stakeholders early and throughout the process.
- Successful REAs are a catalyst for action and transfer of knowledge and skills to local communities.

References

Bhattacharya, Himika. 2008. "New critical collaborative ethnography." In *Handbook of Emergent Methods*, edited by Sharlene Nagy Hesse-Biber and Patricia Leavy, 303–322. New York, NY: The Guilford Press.

Beebe, James. 2001. *Rapid Assessment Process: An Introduction.* Walnut Creek, CA: Alta Mira Press.

Bosk, Charles L., and Raymond G. De Vries. 2004. Bureaucracies of mass deception: Institutional review boards and the ethics of ethnographic research. *The Annals of the American Academy of Political and Social Science* 595(1): 249–263.

Fluehr-Lobban, Carolyn. 1994. Informed consent in anthropological research: We are not exempt. *Human Organization* 52(1): 1–10.

Heimer, Carol and Juleigh Petty. 2010. Bureaucratic ethics: IRBs and the legal regulation of human subjects research. *Annual Review of Law and Social Science* 6(1): 601–626.

Lederman, Rena. 2006. The perils of working at home: IRB "mission creep" as context and content for an ethnography of disciplinary knowledges. *American Ethnologist* 33(4): 482–491.

Lederman, Rena. 2007. "Educate your IRB (A Boilerplate Experiment)." Savage Minds Blog. Accessed September 1, 2019. http://savageminds.org/2007/04/02/educate-your-irb-a-boilerplate-experiment/

Librett, Mitch and Dina Perrone. 2010. Apples and oranges: ethnography and the IRB. *Qualitative Research* 10(6): 729–747.

Miles, Matthew B., A. Michael Huberman, and Johnny Saldaña. 2014. *Qualitative Data Analysis: A Methods Sourcebook*. Thousand Oaks, CA: Sage.

Punch, Maurice. 1994. "The politics and ethics of fieldwork." In *Handbook of Qualitative Research*, edited by Norman K. Denzin and Yvonna S. Lincoln, 83–97. Thousand Oaks, CA: Sage.

Smith, Linda T. 2005. "On tricky ground: Researching the native in the age of uncertainty." In *Handbook of Qualitative Research*, edited by Norman K. Denzin and Yvonna S. Lincoln, 85–107. Thousand Oaks, CA: Sage.

Steneck, Nicholas H. 2007. *ORI Introduction to the responsible conduct of research*. Washington DC: Government Printing Office.

U.S. Department of Health and Human Services. 2018. "What Is a Contract? 5 Differences between Grants and Contracts." Washington DC: Grants.gov Program Management Office. Accessed September 1, 2019. https://blog.grants.gov/2018/05/09/what-is-a-contract-5-differences-between-grants-and-contracts/

Visweswaran, Kamala. 1997. Histories of feminist ethnography. *Annual Review of Anthropology* 26: 591–621.

3 Rapid ethnographic assessment design and methods

Key learning outcomes

1 Identify key aims for the REA
2 Understand how to design a successful REA
3 Choose appropriate methods and sampling strategies for data collection
4 Gain competency in writing field notes

In this chapter, we focus on defining the purpose and need of REAs, and determining key aims and objectives that guide REA design and conduct. Using examples from previously completed REAs, we review methods such as ethnographic observation, ethnographic and geospatial mapping, in-depth key informant interviews, focus groups, and surveys. We also present several sampling frames to keep in mind and discuss the critical importance of writing field notes as part of the data collection process. Finally, we discuss the benefits and complexities of specific methods and offer recommendations for utilizing multiple methods based on REA research questions.

Defining purpose and need

REA is an approach to data collection that can be used for a variety of purposes; among them, exploratory or formative research; as a tool for evaluation, needs assessment, program assessment; or a part of rapid response activities (see Box 3.1). In many instances, REAs are conducted around a research problem on which few studies exist. The focus is on gaining new insights into an emerging situation or existing issue. REA can be used as preliminary research to establish an understanding of how best to proceed in further studying an issue or what more needs to be done to gather information. The goals here are to gain familiarity with a situation, generate new ideas or assumptions, and determine whether additional studies or follow-up is needed. For example, information gathered through REAs used as formative research has been used to generate language and categories necessary in developing standardized surveys.

Box 3.1

REA uses

- Exploratory or formative research
- Project or program evaluation
- Needs assessment
- Program assessment
- Part of rapid response activities

In addition to aiding exploration, assessment, and evaluation, REA's basic approach lends itself to quickly gathering information to change or improve a service or outcome. For example, a social service agency may want to know more about the mental health needs of recently relocated refugees in its service area. Or a food bank may be trying to determine the reasons for a sudden decline in the number of clients they see each week. Perhaps a county health department wants more information about how sexually transmitted disease (STD) services for men who have sex with men (MSM) are organized in order to address a rising epidemic. In all these cases, a combination of rapid qualitative data collection methods carried out by an interdisciplinary team over a relatively short time can yield useful information that can quickly be put to use in making adjustments or tailoring services (see Box 3.2). In this chapter, we will discuss the primary methods used in REAs and illustrate how a combination of these methods, when used together along with techniques inherent in team-based fieldwork and analysis, results in more robust data that lead to actionable findings. In REA, triangulation—the collection and interpretation of data across sources, methods, researchers, and even disciplines—allows for different perspectives

---

Box 3.2

Example: Congenital syphilis in Louisiana

In 2011, the Louisiana Office of Public Health STD/HIV Program requested technical assistance in understanding increases in syphilis and congenital syphilis (CS) among young African American women in Caddo Parish. Specifically, they wanted to: (1) understand community and structural-level factors that may have been contributing to these increases; (2) identify factors that affected access to and use of services to prevent STDs and CS; and (3) solicit recommendations to strengthen services to prevent syphilis and CS. Together, we determined that a REA would be an effective way of obtaining information from women and their providers about the health and social service needs of young African American women. We also agreed that the REA would serve as a needs assessment to identify possible leverage points for intervention.

and vantage points and adds "breadth and depth" to our understanding of a phenomenon (Beebe 2001). In REA, as in other qualitative research, the goal is to obtain and elucidate a range of views and responses, rather than to validate one particular perspective (Beebe 2001).

Determining methods

Qualitative data collection methods form the foundation of REAs, and there are several core methods that are often used in combination. These complementary methods help position REA as a structural, community, and individual-level assessment tool. These include:

- Interviews with participants, some of whom are considered key informants
- Focus groups
- Ethnographic observation
- Mapping
- Brief surveys
- Field notes

The selection of methods depends on various factors including key aims and research questions, needs of the participants, resources, and logistics. Nearly all REAs rely on some form of individual, in-depth interviewing, although parameters for these may vary. Depending on the REA, focus groups may complement interviews to obtain a "group" or "public" perspective. The intimate and private nature of individual interviews allows individuals to share their thoughts, opinions, and experiences more freely. If the topics of discussion are particularly sensitive, in-depth key informant interviews are more appropriate to ensure privacy and confidentiality. However, if one of the goals of the REA is to find out more about group norms or the feasibility of certain interventions in a community, focus groups can be very useful.

Other methods common to REA are ethnographic observations, mapping, and brief surveys. These methods complement or round out interview data and provide additional context for what is being discussed in interviews and focus groups. Finally, field notes, when diligently recorded, create yet another record of what takes place during data collection, capturing not only observations and terminology, but immediate impressions and reflections of field team members as they occur. These methods and how the team uses them to create a robust REA data set will be discussed below and in subsequent chapters. Many qualitative methods are best used in tandem so that they inform a holistic, robust understanding of individual, community, organizational, and structural-level factors related to the research questions of the REA.

In-depth ethnographic interviews

What are in-depth interviews?

Interviews with participants are one-on-one, in-depth discussions to explore perceptions and understandings of problems, behaviors, motivations, and challenges. Interviews also elicit information about everyday experiences and needs. The goal of an in-depth interview is to learn from the participant what they think about a topic in their own words.

Individual interviews create an intimate atmosphere where the participant can discuss their personal views as they relate to a topic. Interviews allow the participant to discuss personal experiences, as well as motivations, opinions, and beliefs about a subject. The key aim of the interviewer during an interview is to learn from participants about their perceptions and thoughts regarding the phenomenon in question by asking open-ended questions, actively listening to responses, and asking follow-up questions based on the responses. This requires listening in a focused way, not just looking for answers. Interviewers should not lead participants to particular answers, or ask questions that elicit "yes," "no," or single-word answers. During the interview itself, for instance, we recommend that the interviewer briefly restate what the participant has said before moving to the next question. This brief summary—just a sentence or two—can help establish rapport during the interview as it signals to the participant that the interviewer is actively listening and has understood what they have discussed (Leech 2002). Repeating participants' answers can also provide a chance for the participant to correct the interviewer if there has been a misunderstanding of the discussion or to elaborate further on a previous response. As an interviewer, it is important to use the participants' own language to summarize and to avoid interpreting their responses as this can leave participants feeling like the interviewer is suggesting they said something that they did not say or mean.

Further, the interviewer should act professionally and as if they are generally familiar with the particular topic of the interview, but less knowledgeable than the participant (Leech 2002). It is critical that the participant not leave out something because they assume the interviewer already knows about it. By creating a setting where the participant is considered the expert, interviewers also facilitate participants' confidence in discussing sensitive matters or disclosing confidential issues. The success of individual interviews is dependent on the ability of the interviewer to establish rapport with the participant (i.e., establishing an environment where the participant feels comfortable and at ease), emphasize the participants' perspective, and probe and prompt as needed.

How do you select participants to interview?

Participants are a group of people with experience and knowledge of the research subject. Participants are also able and willing to talk about the key issues of interest to the REA team. This does not mean they are experts in a formal sense, but that they should have some role or relation to the topic and be willing to talk about it. Participants should represent a wide range of individuals in the affected community. This can mean interviewing decision makers, providers, and community leaders, but it may also mean interviewing individuals with no official role to speak of, such as patients, students, or individuals living in a neighborhood that have an interest in the problem. In REAs, it is important to recruit individuals who are willing to talk with researchers about the issues being investigated and who have a perspective on the topic. One of the goals of REAs is to obtain a diversity of opinions and views and to seek participants who can discuss an issue from different vantage points. Not all participants will be directly affected by the situation being studied, but they may have important things to say about the topic.

How do you construct interview guides for in-depth interviews?

Interview guides and their level of detail should be decided beforehand. Interview guides are designed to help guide interviews and to standardize the collection of information. The emphasis is on creating questions that elicit detailed descriptions or narratives from participants. They are different from questionnaires, which tend to ask survey questions that limit answers to "yes," "no," one-word or sentence, or are worded in a way to influence or limit participants' responses. There are two types of interviews that are possible with participants:

- *Semi-structured:* a type of interview in which there are a few pre-structured questions that guide the flow of the conversation, but which leave much of the discussion unstructured so that the interviewer and participants have the ability to talk about perspectives and attitudes in an unrestricted way. The goal of a semi-structured interview is not to rigidly follow the list of questions, but to guide the conversation to focus on the topics of interest. Semi-structured interviews require a great amount of skill on the part of the interviewer because they must keep the conversation natural, while at the same time directing it to address issues relevant to the research questions.
- *Structured:* a type of interview where questions are predetermined and are adhered to more concretely. Structured interviews ask the same questions in the same order of all participants so that the resulting data is easier to compare across participants. The format may prove too inflexible in some circumstances; for example, when unexpected information may not be recorded because there is no accommodation in the interview framework to allow for responses or information that does not fit within the predetermined structure.

Most REAs will follow a semi-structured interview guide to allow for conversations to proceed naturally but still maintain focus. There are several types of questions that can be used when developing the interview guide for REAs:

- **Descriptive**
  - o Ask a participant to describe something (e.g., Could you describe X?)
- **Experience**
  - o Ask a participant their experience with something (e.g., Can you tell me about your experience with X?)
- **Perception**
  - o Ask a participant their perception of something (e.g., How do you feel, think about X? What is your opinion on X?)
- **Structured**
  - o Output is structured; used to generate lists of things (e.g., What are all the services that your organization provides?)

Constructing questions for an in-depth interview, even if using a semi-structured guide, is important. In REAs, individual interviews typically last from 30–90 minutes, and we recommend developing five to seven key questions beforehand. These questions can then be elaborated on through multiple follow-up questions and probes (see Box 3.3). The interview guide can also be modified, if necessary, based on the first few interviews.

Box 3.3

Constructing inclusive in-depth interview questions

- Ask one question at a time
- Ask open-ended questions

  - o How would you describe...?
  - o What are your thoughts on...?

- Avoid yes/no questions
- Don't ask leading questions

  - o Do you think parents don't talk about sex and condoms because they are too embarrassed?

- Verify/expand unclear answers (probe, follow-up)

  - o Can you please elaborate/give me an example?
  - o What do you mean when you say...?

The structure of a question matters as it may determine the kind of answer received. Using a "grand tour" question as the first question is a standard technique in ethnographic interviewing because it allows the participant, rather than the interviewer, to "set the agenda" and disclose at the beginning of the interview what they think are the major issues (Spradley 1979). A grand tour question encourages participants to talk, frames the interview as a dialogue or conversation, and allows for the emergence of new lines of inquiry related to the topic. It also allows the interviewer to circle back to or follow up on particular questions or topics included in the interview guide that have not already been addressed. Responses to grand tour questions offer the interviewer multiple opportunities for examining more routine aspects of experience. "Can you describe a typical day at work?" or "Can you tell me all the things that happen when you go to the clinic for care?" are examples of grand tour questions.

Question order can also affect interviews. Most REAs are about individual and community perceptions, and starting the interview with a few demographic questions can serve as a neutral and non-threatening way of beginning the interview. These questions also provide the interviewer with some key pieces of data about the participant that may be useful to know for the interview. Sensitive questions should come during the middle or towards the end of the interview.

An important part of interviewing is following up on things participants tell you. The initial question may elicit a response but there may be a need to ask more questions to get the full story. A probe or follow-up question is usually used for a request for additional or more precise, detailed information. For instance, a probe could ask, "Could you give me an example of what happened when you say that your husband got very angry?" or "Who else was with you when you went to that corner to try to buy drugs?" A follow-up question could also be asked to clarify something. For instance, "Could you give me an example of how you used [term or phrase]?" It is often better to ask for use rather than meaning (Spradley 1979; Leech 2002). For instance, following up with questions like "When would you do that?" or "How would you use that?" rather than "What do you mean when you say that?" allows the participant to continue using their own words to describe their perspectives and behavior rather than to shift to an explanatory frame, treating the interviewer like an outsider, using words to translate the situation in a way that the participant thinks the interviewer will understand (Leech 2002).

Logistics of interviews

Ethnographic interviews usually take more time to administer than surveys. Although there is no hard and fast rule, interviews in REAs should generally last 30–90 minutes. Too short and it may be difficult to learn much of any use; too long may weary a participant or take up too much of a participant's busy day. Interviews can be either recorded digitally or through handwritten or typed notes taken during the interview. There are pros and cons to recording interviews. Depending on the time, resources, and scope of the project, REAs may rely on written notes that record what is being said verbatim as much as possible. Obviously, this can be challenging, but if the results of the REA are needed especially quickly, or if resources are low or technology not available, this may be preferable to recording. In our work with state health departments, we seldom used recorders due to the need for quick turnaround and budget considerations. Instead, we developed a protocol for interviewing in which interviewers worked in pairs, with one person acting as the interviewer and the other as a note taker. Before the interview, the interviewer introduced the note taker and explained each person's role (see Box 3.4).

In general, we avoided having both the interviewer and the note taker asking questions at the same time because this can overwhelm a participant. Instead, at the end of the interview, the interviewer asked the note taker if they had any additional questions or follow-ups for the participant. Expansion of the note taker's notes, along with any additional field notes (e.g., observations of behavior and activities, interview reflections) by the interviewer and note taker soon after the interview resulted in a robust, cohesive set of written notes. Our protocol called for the note taker to create a typed "transcript" based on notes, and the interviewer then added to this, fleshing out other details and adding memos with reflections, thoughts, and topics for follow up.

Field notes capture ideas and memories from interviews that may be lost later in the research process. This continual process of observing and writing and making connections within and outside the interview, can be helpful

---

Box 3.4

Example: Interviewing—sex work and migrant men in North Carolina

The semi-structured interview guide was developed during the planning stages; however, additional questions were incorporated iteratively based on new information learned during the interviews. Interview questions were open-ended, exploratory, and designed to elicit participants' views on a range of topics, including perceptions of the typology of sex work, women involved in sex work and their risk for HIV/STD, Latino male clients of sex workers and their risk for HIV/STD, sexual health seeking behaviors, and barriers and facilitators to use of HIV/STD prevention services.

Interviews were not recorded; instead, handwritten notes were taken during the interview by a note taker, and then expanded by the note taker and interviewer after the interview. REA team debriefing occurred daily and after each interview; field notes were taken during these meetings.

for subsequent analysis (Wengraf 2001). However, as with interview notes, handwritten field notes cannot be replayed and can result in a loss of information and details. Expanding field notes (discussed later in the chapter) quickly after interviews or observations can mitigate such disadvantages.

If time and resources allow, using technology to digitally record interviews provides certain advantages, such as being able to replay an interview session unlimited times. Digital recording software can also make it fairly easy to search through interviews for specific excerpts. Transcripts based on digital files, therefore, allow for the data to be retrieved and examined in a more flexible manner (Atkinson and Heritage 1999; Lapadat and Lindsay 1999). Digital recordings and transcriptions, however, add substantial cost and time. For instance, for every hour of a recorded interview, 6–7 hours of transcription are required (Britten 1995). The additional time required for transcription can significantly slow the progression of a REA. Also, transcription errors and loss of information are common, whether they are mistakes made by REA team members or others hired to transcribe. Finally, the logistics of transporting recording equipment and transferring and securing digital files add a level of complexity to some REA projects that must be considered.

Before conducting the interview, the interviewer and note taker should introduce themselves and the project to the participant. The interviewer should explain how privacy will be protected and have the participant sign any necessary consent forms. They should make sure to tell the participant why their views are important. Further, they need to explain how the interview will be conducted (e.g., taking notes, recorded digitally, etc.), clarifying the role of the interviewer as well as that of the note taker. The interviewer and note taker should make the participant feel comfortable (i.e., establish rapport). Finally, the interviewer needs to ask if the participant has any questions before beginning the interview.

During the interview, interviewers should ask questions rather than make statements. They should be sure not to interrupt the participant or finish their sentences. They should often use probes and follow-up questions to clarify what terms mean or ask for more detail. It is also critical that interviewers not state their own judgments or opinions, take over the interview, or center it on their perspectives. Likewise, interviewers should be aware of body language—both their own and the participant's—and avoid non-verbal body reactions as much as possible. Finally, interviewers should never correct what they may think is "wrong" information. If the participant asks for an opinion, the interviewer should politely say they will come back to that at the end of the interview. In a REA, it is a given that the team will be made up of individuals with different types of disciplinary training that will influence their interview styles; awareness of one's own disciplinary style or biases should be part of training interviewers for REA. (see Table 3.1)

Silence can be golden! Interviewers should learn to be comfortable with silence and to use a few seconds to pause. Don't rush the participant: pause

Table 3.1 Style of data collection

What is your data collection style? (adapted from Ulin et al. 2005)		
Training	Strengths	Weaknesses
Health care workers	• Comfort with discussing sexual behaviors, reproductive health issues • Good at engaging people, building trust • Some people are more willing to talk with them because they seem knowledgeable	• Discomfort listening to "wrong" information (tendency to teach rather than listen) • May block free discussion, or come across as authoritarian
Survey researchers	• Conscientious • Careful adherence to protocol • Efficient and careful documentation	• Tendency to be rigid or follow protocol in robotic way • May have difficulty knowing when, how to probe appropriately
Social scientists	• Theoretical and methodological training in qualitative methods • Awareness of cultural assumptions of the interviewer and participant • Oriented toward holistic, systems thinking • Careful documentation of research process and data	• May spend too much time on each data collection task • Devotion to favorite theories • May not understand the nuances of applied research • May have trouble staying focused on stated objectives

for a few seconds after a question is asked and after a participant's comment. Such breaks in conversation give participants—and the interviewer—time to think. Silence also lets the participant know that the interviewer is taking a minute to let them think about the question. At the end of the interview, it is important to ask the participant if they have anything else to add or if they still have any remaining questions about the work being done.

Immediately after the interview has ended, the interviewer should write down notes on the general impressions and assessments of the interview. Translation and transcription of interviews should be done as soon as possible. Interviewing can be exhausting because of the intense focus needed and the time it takes to write up field notes; therefore, most interviewers should aim to conduct no more than 3–4 hours of interviewing per day.

Group interviews

REAs take place quickly and interactions in the field can be unpredictable. On numerous occasions a team arrived for a scheduled individual interview at an agency or program, only to find that additional staff members were invited, unbeknownst to the REA team, to sit in with, or be part of, the individual's interview. At first, we resisted this, insisting that only one person be present for the interview, but over time we realized that these "group" interviews, while tricky to manage, sometimes yielded useful information. For example, a manager or program director sometimes asked clinical staff to sit in and help answer specific questions that a manager could not answer. These impromptu group interviews, are not, however, to be confused with focus groups. Focus groups—their purpose and structure—are discussed below. We recommend that, if possible, a group interview be limited to two to three participants; larger groups can be difficult to manage, and it becomes impossible for a note taker to capture all relevant content.

Focus groups

What is a focus group?

A focus group (sometimes referred to as a focus group discussion) is an interview of a group of people about an issue (see Box 3.5). Focus groups use group interaction to produce data and insights that would be difficult to do without group interaction. In focus groups, the interview takes place in a group setting and includes individuals who come from similar backgrounds and have shared experiences. Focus groups are different from interviews in that individuals in a focus group are talking to each other as well as the focus group facilitator. They are also different from participant/direct observation because individuals in a focus group are talking about topics introduced by the focus group facilitator rather than those that are naturally generated. Notes from the focus groups and any recordings, like interviews, need to be translated and transcribed immediately or as soon as possible.

Box 3.5

When to use a focus group

- When there is a need to learn about "public" norms or values in a community
- When group interaction and debate about a topic is useful
- When time is limited and there is a need to gather data quickly from a group of people
- When there is a need to review an intervention and gather perspectives on how to improve it
- When the topic of discussion can be freely discussed in a group without embarrassment or concerns

---

When are focus groups useful?

Focus groups allow observation of interactions between participants and group discussion, which can help shed light on topics on which very little information exists. Focus groups can also be very useful in determining feasibility of certain interventions or gaining a better understanding of research findings gathered through other methods. Focus groups can be cost-effective and save time because they enable researchers to gather large amounts of data relatively quickly. Focus groups are often used to expand on or further explore aspects of topics in REAs, complementing what is learned through interviews. Focus groups rarely take the place of interviews in REAs. For example, in a large, multi-site REA that explored the HIV prevention needs of female sex workers and clients, data collection called for both interviews and focus groups. Interviews explored individual women's personal experience of sex work, sexual practices, and interactions with clients, whereas focus groups were geared to understand local terminology, emerging changes in the market for sex, and the accessibility of services for women's health. The latter topics generated discussion among women and provided additional context but were not as sensitive as those covered in interviews.

What are key considerations in planning and conducting focus groups?

There are some situational challenges in conducting a focus group. Depending on the target group, setting, and topic, some people may not want to participate in a focus group because they may not want to associate with or be seen by other individuals in particular settings. It can also be a challenge to discuss illicit and stigmatizing behaviors in a group setting, where some participants may give answers that they consider publicly acceptable rather than discuss their own attitudes and behaviors. In the example above, it may not have been productive to ask female sex workers about their individual strategies for negotiating prices for sex acts during a focus group, because some women may be reluctant to reveal this information to women they considered competitors.

REA planners should try to ensure that participants in any one focus group have something in common with each other that is related to the key aims of the REA. People generally talk more openly if they are in a group of people who share the same background or experiences. Although differences can often make for a lively debate, revealing contrasting and sometimes important perspectives, this can also backfire if some people in the focus group feel reluctant to share their views. For example, if the team is interested in learning more about sexual practices among women, it may be disadvantageous to include both young single women and older married women in the same focus group. Young women may feel obliged to discuss "acceptable" practices rather than their true range of experiences and behaviors in front of older women. Participants with different backgrounds and experience can restrict the openness of discussion within the focus group. Given this, characteristics of focus group participants need to be considered in terms of which factors might most influence more open discussion among participants. It is not a given that focus group participants should be from the same demographic or ethnic group, but these characteristics should be considered among other factors that are relevant to the project.

After deciding who should be included in the focus groups, the number of focus groups needs to be determined. Multiple focus groups can occur based on the same topic to elicit different perspectives. For instance, in a study of satisfaction with school administration, focus group discussions could be conducted with school staff, parents, and students separately. The number of focus groups depends on project objectives, time, and resources. Again, it is good practice to conduct the fewest number of focus groups needed to achieve variability, and to do them well, rather than conduct many focus groups poorly.

The number of participants within a focus group should ideally be between five and ten people, although focus groups with as few as four sometimes suffice. A group that is too small may lack the diversity of perspectives or interactions that generate discussion. Groups with more than eight can be difficult to manage. That said, the decision as to how many participants you want in each focus group will depend on how a particular community conducts discussions in natural community settings. Because REAs often take place quickly and in settings with few resources, the team may sometimes find itself interacting with larger community groups in more public settings (e.g., community meeting, board meeting). Although these kinds of opportunistic discussions may not conform to all the parameters of focus groups, they can still be quite useful. As in the discussion of group interviews above, these interactions should not be confused with focus groups, and REA teams should be clear and transparent when reporting how data were collected.

Many researchers who use focus groups advocate for them as a stand-alone method in data collection. However, as stated above, we do not recommend the exclusive use of focus groups. Other kinds of information, particularly around social and cultural context, are necessary to understand and interpret focus group discussion.

What is the role of the facilitator?

Facilitating focus group discussions requires managing personalities as well as time. The focus group facilitator must handle the discussion so that all participants have an opportunity to speak and the group is not dominated by just a few speakers, while at the same time keeping the flow of discussion natural.

This does not mean going around a circle and asking everyone to give an answer. On the contrary, the best focus group data often comes from thoughtful give-and-take among participants, with the focus group facilitator guiding the conversation when needed. The facilitator also must be mindful of time limits and keep the discussion moving so that all desired topics are covered. As in interviews, covering fewer topics well is preferable to covering many topics superficially or peripherally. Creating this balance takes training and experience, and often a skilled facilitator experienced in qualitative social science research methods will be able to clearly outline interview topics and questions and share techniques for managing focus groups, if not conducting the group themselves.

Brief surveys

Sometimes it is necessary or beneficial to collect survey data for REAs. Surveys can take multiple forms, but the most common types of surveys used in REAs include those which are brief questionnaires designed to collect information such as socio-demographics, institutional capacity, and service use (Needle et al. 2003).

In almost all REAs, some demographic data such as age, gender, ethnicity, or education are collected to characterize the interview sample. However, these data are minimal in nature, consisting of five to ten questions. Professional roles or training of participants may be relevant to what is discussed, so these data may be collected. In planning for the collection of these data, consider what approvals may be necessary; some Institutional Review Board (IRB) and US Office of Management and Budget (OMB) approval processes may require separate submission and approvals for what they consider "survey" data. Therefore, it may be advantageous to ask only a few questions and incorporate these into the REA interview guide.

A street-intercept survey is another type of survey often used in a REA. It involves asking individuals in key locations (e.g., healthcare venues, events, restaurants, conferences, and shopping malls) about topics relevant to the research question. The survey is very brief (usually no more than five minutes) and is typically conducted where the individual is intercepted. During an intercept survey, the interviewer may approach an individual to ask about their experience at the event or facility. Street intercepts may be used, for example, to learn if people in a particular area are aware of a health department communications campaign about a disease outbreak. Results from the intercept surveys allow the client organization to obtain feedback from their target audience while the information is still fresh in their minds. Intercept surveys should be in done in different areas of the proposed survey area, based on initial information about various communities. Advantages of this method are that it is quick, non-threatening, and easy to do. As such, they can yield high response rates from hard-to-reach populations. Street intercepts have value in that they complement and can be triangulated with other types of data such as interviews and observations.

Sampling—who should we talk to and how do we find them?

In a REA, the key objective is to understand local perspectives and categorize the issues under investigation. Ethnographic researchers seek "saturation," meaning *how many* isn't the issue. Better questions to ask are "Do you understand the phenomenon? Have you learned enough?" Saturation is typically reached when no new information is forthcoming from additional data collection. Mere numbers of interviews are irrelevant; deep understanding is the goal. As a result, the preference is to cover fewer cases in an in-depth manner rather than cover many cases in a cursory manner.

When designing a REA, the focus should be on including a variety of participants who are known to have in-depth knowledge and experience in the areas being investigated (see Box 3.6). This does not mean that

---

Box 3.6

Example: Sampling—congenital syphilis (CS) in Louisiana

During a one-week REA to learn more about the context of CS increases in a Louisiana parish, we used purposive and snowball sampling. We contacted state and local HIV/STD program staff by phone before arriving in Louisiana. We also identified other organizations and individuals who might have relevance for the assessment through referrals from local program staff and our own literature search before beginning the REA. These potential participants were then contacted by phone, informed about the purpose of the REA and asked if they would be willing to participate in a one-hour open-ended interview during the assessment week. We also asked them to refer other individuals or organizations that provide services to vulnerable women to us.

Over a period of four days during which we conducted our REA, a total of 69 persons participated in 35 separate interviews; 23 of these were conducted as one-on-one interviews and 12 were carried out as group (coded as 1+ persons) interviews or discussions. Of the 69 individual participants, 58 were female and 11 were male; 32 were African American and 37 were white. Interviews or discussions included 14 that took place at community-based organizations, including community-based clinics; 11 at or with staff from public and private hospitals or clinics; 6 at the Parish Health Unit; 2 in correctional settings; 1 at a church; and 1 at a school of nursing. Participants represented a diverse cross-section of persons who provide health and other services to adolescent and young adult African American women, including social workers; primary, prenatal, and STD health care providers; outreach workers; disease intervention specialists; educators; and community leaders. Two group interviews were held with women in the community—one with teen mothers and one with adult women at a homeless shelter.

only experts should be included; on the contrary, participants should ideally represent a range of perspectives, views, beliefs, values, and behaviors found in the target areas as a whole. In health-related REAs, for example, participants can include (1) economic, policy, and community leaders, (2) health and social service managers and providers, (3) individuals from vulnerable and affected populations who may need or use services, and (4) individuals living in the targeted geographic areas. Having a range of participants allows for in-depth analysis of important concepts and ideas related to the key aims of the REA as well as an opportunity to assess the range of alternative concepts and ideas.

In all research projects, decisions must be made about which individuals to include, whether conducting REA or a large survey. Sampling is a method used to select particular individuals, locales, or organizations to include in the research because it is not possible to identify and communicate with every member of the target community due to limited time and resources. Sampling allows those conducting research to infer information about a population based on results from their sample.

Several different sampling techniques are available, and they are often subdivided into two groups: *probability sampling* and *non-probability sampling* (Collins, Onwuegbuzie, and Jiao 2007). Probability or random sampling is often used in quantitative research, where you start with a complete sampling frame of all eligible individuals from which you select your sample. The rationale behind probability sampling is that each individual has an equal opportunity of being chosen for the sample, and this allows for better generalizations of study results. Because they involve large samples, probability sampling methods tend to be more time-consuming and expensive than non-probability sampling. Several types of probability sampling methods exist: random sampling, stratified sampling, systematic sampling, cluster random sampling, and multi-stage sampling.

Like most research that employs mainly qualitative or mixed methods, REAs use non-probability sampling because the focus is on understanding local perspectives and the intricacies of the local context, rather than to make statistical inferences or generalizations from the sample being studied to the wider population of interest. In qualitative research, there is no correct way to determine how many individuals to recruit. Often, data are collected until a point of theoretical saturation is reached, where the research team is no longer hearing, seeing, or learning new information. Non-probability sampling includes convenience sampling, purposive sampling, quota sampling, snowball sampling, or a combination of these sampling strategies.

In REAs, the most suitable sampling methods include purposive and snowball sampling, which are often used together. *Opportunistic* or *purposive sampling* entails identifying and selecting individuals, communities, or organizations that are especially knowledgeable about or experienced with a phenomenon of interest. Purposive samples are comprised of not just those who are knowledgeable and experienced, but also available, willing, and able to communicate perspectives and experiences. Purposive sampling includes accessing and working with individuals of a target population using opportunities as they arise. Community gatekeepers, who may hold formal or informal roles in the community, are defined as individuals who "control access to information, other individuals and settings" (Schensul et al. 1999). These individuals can prove helpful in this kind of sampling because they can open up channels to communicate with and recruit other constituents in their social networks. Purposive sampling is useful in corroborating the existence and frequency of particular issues that place certain individuals at risk for harm. But it can also lead to the accessing of only the most visible individuals in the target population.

Snowball sampling is a suitable technique to use when target populations are hidden or highly stigmatized. This type of methodology relies heavily on individuals who act as intermediaries and introduce investigators to participants. For instance, an individual who is known to be of the target population is contacted and links the research team with others in their social network. These participants in turn can provide the research team with more members from their social networks or target sample.

Sampling is more than just a technical phase of research; it is a necessary and important feature of research design. It signifies a relational moment, where the type of contact between researcher(s) and participants is conceptualized—and potentially later embodied (Noy 2008). It also illustrates that sampling and the data collection methods that are employed are intimately related rather than separated phases of research. For instance, the use of snowball sampling for generating interviews can reveal a lot about social hierarchies within a given community, individual social networks, and the strength of interpersonal relationships in a given context.

Ethnographic observation

What is ethnographic observation?

In ethnographic research, observing daily or routine activities is essential to investigating diverse perspectives within a community or a setting (Spradley 2016). Ethnographic observation always occurs in a field setting and within locations that are relevant to the research questions. Observation allows the researcher to observe participants in their own environment rather than having participants come to the researcher. Ideally, ethnographic observation allows the researcher to learn what it is like to be an "insider" while still maintaining her status as an "outsider."

Observation not only requires awareness of the interactions between people, places, and things, but also how these interactions relate to the larger issues being studied. By observing everyday actions and conversations, researchers gain an understanding of the social, political, and economic contexts in which participants live, work, and play; the relations between people and their environments; and peoples' behaviors and actions.

Why is ethnographic observation useful?

Observational data serve to compare and contrast participants' subjective views of their actions and beliefs. Observational data also provides context for understanding data collected through other types of methods in a REA. For instance, researchers may follow up to do structured observations of a street corner where participants have indicated that a high volume of sex work occurs. Or they may use observational field notes of interactions between clinic staff to supplement interview data discussing contentious interactions between clinic administrators and nurses.

How do I conduct ethnographic observation?

Ethnographic observation in the field requires more than looking and taking field notes; it is a focused and structured way of seeing and listening to what is going on in an environment. Researchers need to be prepared to adapt to a variety of settings and observe and interact with people as they engage in activities in settings such as bars, parks, streets, and homes. Observations can be done by individual researchers or teams, as appropriate for covering the locations and topics of interest. The REA team may learn of observation sites through interviews and focus groups with key informants or through their background research. Observations can be done at any point of the research and is highly dependent on the needs of the project. What, whom, and where to observe is highly variable, but should always have the goal of helping to illustrate or document activities, places, or behaviors germane to the research. Observations can be collected in different locations at different times to get a variety of perspectives. For example, if the team is observing clinic activity, observations should be taken at different times of the day and days of the week. In all cases, the presence of observers should be *discreet* enough to not interrupt the observed environment but *open* enough not to compromise participants' privacy. We will discuss this below in further detail.

What do I document in ethnographic observations?

Clear outlines of what, when, and whom to observe help guide observations. At the same time, remember to be flexible so that unexpected verbal and non-verbal interactions also get recorded. Before conducting observations, think about the following:

- What do we want to learn about people?
    - ○ Who are they? What are they like?
    - ○ Where do they live, work, and play?
    - ○ What are the relationships between different individuals and groups?

- What do we want to learn about behaviors and activities?

  o What is happening?
  o When is it happening? How frequently is it happening?
  o Where is it happening? Under what context is it happening?
  o Who does what? Who is doing what with whom?

Mapping

Ethnographic mapping

Ethnographic mapping of activities and populations of interest is another useful method in REA. In ethnographic mapping researchers use hand-drawn and computerized maps, drawings, and pictures to understand the environment in which activities take place, from the perspective of participants see Figures 3.1 and 3.2. It is a process of locating, in geospatial terms, places of key activities and the locations of people. Locations and boundaries have meaning and value in terms of how participants view them, and they may not necessarily be recognized by outsiders. For example, some locations may be known to local people as places where hidden activities such as sex work or drug markets take place. A city park may be known locally as territory controlled by one social group as opposed to another. These locations will not appear on a standard map and may not be meaningful in terms of electronic mapping, as they may be fluid, depending on circumstances.

Ethnographic mapping is different from electronic mapping programs in that maps can be spatial, incorporating the geographical and social organizations of a community or a location; but they can also illuminate social networks, showing the various relations between people and groups (Kwan 2002). The key

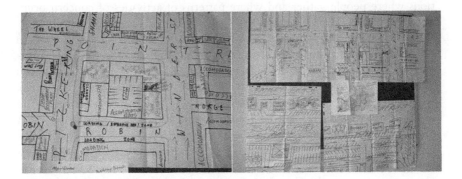

Figure 3.1 Ethnographic maps—South Africa.

Achrekar, Angeli. 2005. "Sex, Drugs, and Deportation: A Rapid Assessment of Drug Use and HIV Risk Patterns of Injecting and Non-Injecting Drug Users in Durban, South Africa." Presentation, International Experience and Technical Assistance (IETA) Final Workshop, December 13, 2005.

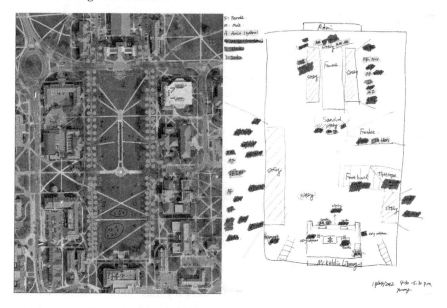

Figure 3.2 Ethnographic maps—Maryland, USA.

Cromer, Caitlin, Charlene Gatewood, Yurong He, and Margaret Wadsworth. 2012. Understanding Diversity on McKeldin Mall. ANTH606: Qualitative Methods in Applied Anthropology Final Paper, University of Maryland.

component of ethnographic mapping is collecting descriptive, in-depth, information pertaining to sites and people. Products are not just maps, showing the locations of people and activities but also include data on underlying social, economic, and environmental factors. Ethnographic mapping can help plan intervention activities in communities because the research team can map locations where people gather and where patterns of activities of concern occur most frequently (Tripathi et al. 2010).

Ethnographic mapping requires involvement of community members. In REA, community members can help identify the best locations for interviews and observations to take place. In a large REA of sex work in South Africa, for example, REA teams spent weeks mapping locations where sex work and drug activity take place (e.g. "hotspots") so that sites for recruiting interview participants could be identified and established before the REA began. Mapping allows frequent communication and interactions with community members and participants. REA team members can ask participants to help co-create lists or locations of key groups, activities; visit locations, or places together; co-sketch maps of places visited; revisit areas to interview about specific activities; and confirm mutually created maps. The REA team can use interviews and observations to refine preliminary map sketches with background information about sites, populations, and activities before transferring sketch maps to a composite map. Anthropology students, for instance, used in-depth interviews and participant observation to clarify and fine-tune ethnographic maps that detailed how public spaces on campus were being used by various groups of students, faculty, and staff.

Before mapping, decide where, when, and how mapping activities will occur. These questions will be helpful in the process of mapping:

• What do we want to learn about the location(s) of interest?

    ○ Where is it (in relation to other places)?
    ○ What is the layout?
    ○ Who are the people, places, and things that inhabit this location? What activities take place here? At what time?
    ○ How do people move in and out of the location?
    ○ How do people relate to each other in this location?
    ○ When and how frequently do interactions occur?

Electronic mapping

Electronic mapping using geographical information systems (GIS) and Google Earth programs can be beneficial in the logistical planning of REAs. These programs can capture and present data with reference to geographic location data and are tools that allow for the generation of interactive searches and analysis of spatial information (e.g., various maps, aerial photos, road and street labels, and other features related to mapping) (Steinberg and Steinberg 2015). Electronic mapping programs can generate maps of potential agency contacts and locations for ethnographic mapping. For several REAs conducted with state and local health departments, we mapped as part of logistical planning, and mapped again in reporting out where agencies were located and interviews took place. For a REA that investigated STD services in urgent care centers (UCC) in a metro area, we used geographic mapping of epidemiological data to help narrow down and locate UCCs for the interview sample (Williams et al. 2019).

REA teams can also use electronic and ethnographic mapping to triangulate information. For instance, anthropology students used GIS mapping to locate grocery stores near campus, and then triangulated this information with ethnographic maps showing where students purchased food items. This allowed them to understand that even without nearby grocery stores, students were able to procure food items, albeit limited, for daily consumption. It also provided them with compelling information to present to university officials regarding the general lack of food options for students living on campus.

Photographs

Photographs can also be used to document key places and spaces that are important to the REA. This could include street corners, housing, meeting spaces, stores, playgrounds, and other important locations. These kinds of images can have many different uses in a REA. For example, we used photographs to document different locations where sex work reportedly took place in North Carolina including truck stops, streets, motels, trailers, housing complexes, clubs, and casinos. In another REA, we used photographs to document how recent cuts to funding impacted STI services, recording, for instance, posted signs of new reduced clinic hours and closings. Photography, like ethnographic mapping, can record key landmarks, places, and locations of communities and groups by discussing them with participants to document sites, people, or cultural landscapes. Likewise, these photographs can be used in ethnographic interviews to "walk" through a particular site or landscape with a participant who has a close connection to a place. This can result in a deeper conversation about the significance or meaning of places and spaces than discussing these contexts without the use of such visual materials (Pink 2013).

Field notes

What are field notes?

Field notes are data resulting from a variety of REA activities, including direct and participant observations done in the field. Field notes constitute detailed descriptions of behaviors, activities, events, discussion, and other features of observations undertaken by those conducting the REA. Field notes can also be taken during interviews and focus group sessions to record non-verbal communication or context under which interviews take place. Field notes are also taken during REA activities such as mapping, surveys, and debriefings to record context and describe impressions, activities, and dialogue. Field notes are intended to be read by the REA team as evidence to give meaning and provide understanding of the context or phenomenon being studied. The notes supplement other data such as those gathered from interviews, focus groups, mapping, and surveys.

How do you take field notes?

It is important to remember to write field notes on an ongoing basis, at the end of observational periods, and during individual interviews, focus groups, or any other type of situation that is relevant to the REA. Learning is a continual process, and therefore it is important for team members to write field notes as they are seeing, hearing, and processing things. REA team members should record data at *all* times, whether at informal meetings or during interviews, focus groups, and field observations. Every moment of data collection should be considered to be an opportunity to write field notes. Field notes should be written even if interviews, focus groups, or observations are being digitally recorded because they serve as a back-up for any recording failures and capture non-verbal communication and behavior. Because there is so much information that is necessary to record during a REA, it is impossible to keep account of everything without having it written down.

These notes should try to capture as much as possible because often, these are the only recording of data that may be possible at a particular site. When preparing field notes, make clear how you come to know something. *Did you see it? Were you told it?* Further, include things that participants said and did to which others responded and reacted. Writing descriptive accounts is not as easy as it appears because it is not transparent or straightforward. Writing field notes is not simply about passively writing down facts; rather, it is the active process of interpreting and sense-making (Emerson, Fretz, and Shaw 2011). There is no one "correct" way to write observations; different descriptions of the same events are possible.

During data collection and fieldwork, REA team members should try to record descriptive information such as verbal and non-verbal communication such as phrases, keywords and concepts, eye contact, pauses, voice tones, laughter, movement, interactions, etc. It is important to write what people actually *say*, verbatim as much as possible. Make sure to capture slang, special terms (e.g., "working the pouches") as well as memorable quotes (e.g., "Budget cuts have been brutal. People are dying."). Avoid interpreting or summarizing. Let participants' words and actions *show* what is happening (see Box 3.7).

Field notes should also record physical setting or social context. For instance, if observation is occurring during a meeting, notes on where the meeting is taking place, who is present, the purpose of the meeting, and the ensuing dialogue and interactions should all be recorded. Reflective information should also be recorded. Be sure to note impressions, reflections, and thoughts (e.g., "The waiting room was full."). Additionally, make notes on things to follow up on (e.g., "The nurse said they can't get the medication that they need to prescribe to the patient.").

Using written notes may be a challenge in some settings such as field observations because it interferes with the act of observation itself and because the people who are being observed may not feel comfortable while having an observer actively writing notes while observing them. In cases where

---

Box 3.7

Field notes: Example

Non-descriptive field notes
"The client was really hostile."

Descriptive field notes
"When Judy...told the client that she could not just do whatever she wanted to do, the client began to yell, screaming that Judy couldn't control her life and then told her to go to hell. The client stomped out of the room and Judy was standing there with her mouth open, looking amazed."

Box 3.8

Field notes: What to write down

- Initial impressions (setting, senses)
- Key events and incidents
- Detailed actions and talk
- Non-verbal communication
- Interactions not individual motivations
- Concerns and perspectives of those in the setting
- General impressions and feelings
- Variations and similarities
- Notes, follow-up questions

---

recording of data is not possible, always make sure to record impressions, observations, and direct quotes as soon as possible (see Box 3.8).

In some settings, a small laptop or tablet might be feasible and not seem obtrusive within certain settings (e.g., interview, meeting, professional settings, etc.). However, this is not always the case. It is always a good idea to carry a notebook or notepad to record field notes. We highly recommend the latter method—taking handwritten field notes.

Making sure everything is written down is not possible (that is, it is an unrealistic expectation). Shorthand simplifies and shortens the field note taking process. Without at least some basic shorthand skills, taking notes in the field can be tricky. Choose a shorthand style that makes sense to you, practice it if you need to, and this will make taking field notes much easier.

How do you expand field notes?

Expanding field notes is a team-based activity for interviews in which the interviewer and note taker sit together and review the interview in order to expand and supplement what each has heard (see Box 3.9). This should take place as soon after the interview as possible, and results in a fuller, more

---

Box 3.9

Field notes: Basic information to include

- Date, time, and location of data collection
- Description of location
- Name/s (pseudonym) of persons interviewed or people observed
- Field team members' names/roles
- Comments on the quality of data collection, setting, etc.
- Number/code for interview/observation

---

elaborated set of notes. Field notes can also be expanded by individual REA team members or by team members collectively for other methods such as observations and mapping. Notes need to be expanded to include rich, in-depth descriptions of what REA team members saw and heard. They should be elaborated from initial descriptions either by hand or electronically (see Figure 3.3). Expansion of notes should occur as soon as possible, usually within 24 hours, because there is more chance that observations and other things not captured in the initial notes will be remembered and recorded. Avoid glossing over information or summarizing. Rather, provide rich details, aiming to show rather than tell. Try, as much as possible, to use a narrative framework, describing what you heard and saw to write expanded field notes including placing verbatim statements in quotes. Writing rich detailed field notes is particularly important as these notes become the raw or source data for analysis and interpretation.

Photographs as field notes

Photographs can be used during fieldwork to record various details such as clinic waiting rooms or health education posters. They are great complements to field notes. Sometimes it is easier to use a camera, particularly a camera phone, to point and shoot an object or place to help remember an incident or context to record later that you might otherwise forget. They are useful when expanding field notes and to facilitate discussion during team debriefings. These photographs do not have to be technically perfect since their main purpose is for recording data—providing details, information, or context. It is important to remember, however, that any data

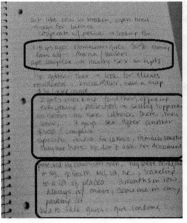

"Seven or eight years ago, the Dominican girls started coming. They were living in apartment complexes. They looked for clients where the clients are living. They had maps and they would go door to door. They actually knock on the doors." A vast majority of these women (90%) were coming from NY, primarily from the Bronx and Harlem.

He says the Dominican girls charge $30 for intercourse—there are usually two girls working together. Sometimes they act like they are offering something else for sale, like Tupperware and they would have sex with one guy after another. They could make on average $300 per apartment complex. They target places or apartment complexes where Latinos live. Families sometimes live there because these apartment complexes do not ask for documentation.

He says that the women were being protected by Dominican men and were sex workers in NYC, and they would travel to Maryland, Virginia, North Carolina, New York City during the year—they don't live here for more than 3 months in a row. He thinks that about half of the women travel down from New York and about half of them stay [live?] here in the area. When they go door to door there's always a guy in the car waiting outside. He has tried to approach the women through the guys but the guys don't let him approach or interact with the women. He was however able to give the guy condoms. He says that once a guy sitting in the car told him that the women were "clean" and that they were "certified and screened in NYC" by the health department. He says the guy showed him what looked to be an ID or registration card.

Figure 3.3 Field note examples.

Images courtesy of the authors.

captured by camera phones may not be secure or confidential. Therefore, we recommend that the REA team establish procedures to make sure that ethical guidelines are being followed at all times to ensure the safety and security of participants.

Team interactions during data collection

The strength of REA lies in team-based interaction and triangulation. These fundamental concepts and practices are key to successful REAs. They ensure that the REA team includes a variety of disciplinary training and content expertise so that multiple perspectives are brought to bear on a problem. Triangulation across interviewers, data sources, and data collection methods further increases the likelihood that an issue will be examined from as many angles as possible. As shown in this chapter, team-based interviewing and observations and expansion of field notes are part of a structured approach that draws on the power of group interaction to offset some of the challenges of rapid ethnographic data collection (see Figure 3.4). In the following chapter, we will discuss the characteristics of a well-rounded REA team, along with additional team-based REA methods that contribute to a successful REA.

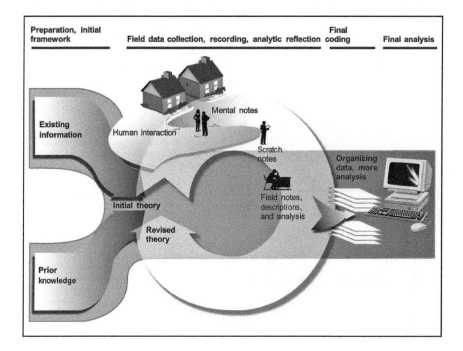

Figure 3.4 The ethnographic research process.

Source: United States General Accounting Office 2003.

Ethics

Ethnographic observation entails research in which ethical issues may develop in real time and space. When conducting observation during REA, team members need to be aware of potential ethical dilemmas and personal biases that may color their relationships with participants and influence their perceptions of what they are observing (see Table 3.2). Observation, as with other methods, is not value-neutral, and the process of observation itself is

Table 3.2 Potential challenges and solutions in interviewing

Challenge	Solution
A participant you are interviewing states obviously incorrect information about the topic. Your first impulse is to correct them.	Do not correct or offer information to the participant during the interview. Instead, let the interview proceed. At the end of the interview, depending on the topic, you may be able to share factual information through brochures, websites, or other sources.
A participant you are interviewing about sexual practices asks you during the interview to explain how syphilis is transmitted.	Let the participant know you will be happy to discuss that at the end of the interview, but for now you'd like to continue. Do not interrupt the flow of the interview to answer questions or explain things. A good practice is to always end an interview by asking if the participant has any questions.
You are conducting an interview and a participant asks for money to buy food.	Do not give a participant money. Refer the participant to other services, if available.
You are interviewing sex workers and a male client enters the room and starts flirting with you in a sexually suggestive way.	Plan ahead. Do not conduct interviews alone in a place that may be unsafe. Maintain your professional boundaries. Immediately leave a situation that becomes uncomfortable for you.
You are conducting street intercepts and a group of young people who are drinking invite you to join them.	Be clear about your boundaries. Politely decline and move to another area.
You and another team member are scheduled to meet a participant at night in an area known as a place to buy drugs. Your team member gets sick and drops out.	Do not go alone. Find another team member or postpone the activity.
You are interviewing in a high school program for pregnant teens. You dress in a formal manner, wear all your best jewelry, and lay your $1200 I-Phone XS on the table in front of you.	Do not wear or display expensive jewelry or technology. Dress simply and appropriately.
A program manager pulls you aside to ask you what their staff talked about in the interviews.	Let the program manager know that each interview is confidential and that you cannot discuss what is said in the interviews due professional and ethical considerations.

enmeshed in the very structural forces and logics of power which the REA is trying to examine. Therefore, it can be highly charged with ethical dilemmas, uncertainties, and responsibilities for which the REA team needs to be prepared.

Before conducting observation, you need to ask whether you need permission from anyone to carry out observation in your setting and whether you need to inform those in the setting where you are observing that you are conducting a REA. There are circumstances, such as observing a workplace or a support group, where it is advisable or required to get permission from someone in charge of the setting (e.g., program manager, lead counselor). In such settings, it is important to be reflective of how the ethics of informed consent may unfold. For instance, some people may not want to be recorded or may feel pressured to take part because an employer or some other gatekeeper has authorized the study. It may be necessary to establish observational parameters for the group or place being studied and to seek permission from individuals as well as gatekeepers. If conducting observational research in public places (e.g., school board meeting, job recruitment fair), it may not be necessary to obtain specific types of permission because it might not be reasonably possible to seek consent from all the individuals entering that space. However, it may also be a good idea to let relevant organizations know that research is being conducted.

There may be times where team members may observe something that gives cause for concern (e.g., illegal activity, abusive language, physical violence). In such instances, be clear about the legal and ethical responsibilities regarding what may be observed during the research and what may or may not be reported. Sometimes, REA team members live in the communities that are being observed or studied or have close relations with the people within these communities or contexts. This can engender a high level of uncertainty and complexity of social interactions in the field as boundaries of researcher and research can become blurry and complicated. For instance, a team member may be reluctant to record illicit items in their field notes in order to protect participants from being reported to authorities, or unconsciously overlook hearing compromising information because it could bring negative attention to an organization or community.

Similar issues may arise during interviews. For instance, a REA in which program staff are acting as interviewers may put them in a position to interview individuals such as program or budget managers. This power differential, although not directly relevant to the REA topic, may create an uncomfortable situation for both. This may sometimes lead to unconscious or deliberate self-censorship where negative community, institutional, or interpersonal dynamics may not be recorded because they present a discouraging picture.

> **Box 3.10**
>
> **Summary**
>
> - REAs can be used for a variety of purposes.
> - Qualitative data collection methods form the foundation of REAs, and can include interviews, observations, mapping, and surveys.
> - The selection of methods for a REA depends on key aims, research questions, participant needs, resources, and logistics.
> - Because the focus of a REA is on including a variety of participants who have in-depth knowledge and experience in the areas being examined, purposive sampling is often used to select which individuals, locales, or organizations to include in the assessment.
> - Field notes constitute detailed descriptions of what is observed by REA team members and must be done on an ongoing basis during data collection.

References

Atkinson, J. Maxwell and John Heritage. 1999. Transcript notation—Structures of social action: studies in conversation analysis. *Aphasiology* 13(4–5): 243–249.

Achrekar, Angeli. 2005. "Sex, Drugs, and Deportation: A Rapid Assessment of Drug Use and HIV Risk Patterns of Injecting and Non-Injecting Drug Users in Durban, South Africa." Presentation, International Experience and Technical Assistance (IETA) Final Workshop, December 13, 2005.

Beebe, James. 2001. *Rapid Assessment Process: An Introduction.* Walnut Creek, CA: Altamira Press.

Britten, Nicky. 1995. Qualitative research: qualitative interviews in medical research. *BMJ* 311(6999): 251–253.

Collins, Kathleen M. T., Anthony J. Onwuegbuzie, and Qun G. Jiao. 2007. A mixed methods investigation of mixed methods sampling designs in social and health science research. *Journal of Mixed Methods Research* 1(3): 267–294.

Cromer, Caitlin, Charlene Gatewood, Yurong He, and Margaret Wadsworth. 2012. Understanding Diversity on McKeldin Mall. ANTH606: Qualitative Methods in Applied Anthropology Final Paper, Department of Anthropology, University of Maryland.

Emerson, Robert M., Rachel I. Fretz, and Linda L. Shaw. 2011. *Writing Ethnographic Fieldnotes.* Chicago, IL: University of Chicago Press.

Kwan, Mei-Po. 2002. Feminist visualization: Re-envisioning GIS as a method in feminist geographic research. *Annals of the Association of American Geographers* 92(4): 645–661.

Lapadat, Judith C., and Anne C. Lindsay. 1999. Transcription in research and practice: From standardization of technique to interpretive positionings. *Qualitative Inquiry* 5(1): 64–86.

Leech, Beth L. 2002. Asking questions: Techniques for semi-structured interviews. *PS: Political Science & Politics* 35(4): 665–668.

Needle, Richard H., Robert T. Trotter, Merrill Singer, Christopher Bates, J. Bryan Page, David Metzger, and Louis H. Marcelin. 2003. Rapid assessment of the HIV/AIDS crisis in racial and ethnic minority communities: an approach for timely community interventions. *American Journal of Public Health* 93(6): 970–979.

Noy, Chaim. 2008. Sampling knowledge: The hermeneutics of snowball sampling in qualitative research. *International Journal of Social Research Methodology* 11(4): 327–344.

Pink, Sarah. 2013. *Doing Visual Ethnography*. Thousand Oaks, CA: Sage.

Schensul, Stephen L., Jean J. Schensul, and Margaret Diane LeCompte. 1999. *Essential Ethnographic Methods*. Walnut Creek, CA: Altamira Press.

Spradley, James P. 1979. *The Ethnographic Interview*. New York, NY: Holt, Rinehart and Winston.

Spradley, James P. 2016. *Participant Observation*. Longrove, IL: Waveland Press.

Steinberg, Shiela L., and Steven J. Steinberg. 2015. *GIS Research Methods: Incorporating Spatial Perspectives*. Redlands, CA: Esri Press.

Tripathi, Binu M., Harendra Kumar Sharma, Pertti J. Pelto, and Shalini Mani Tripathi. 2010. Ethnographic mapping of alcohol use and risk behaviors in Delhi. *AIDS and Behavior* 14(Suppl 1): 94–103.

Ulin, Priscilla R., Elizabeth T. Robinson, and Elizabeth R. Tolley. 2005. *Qualitative Methods in Public Health: A Field Guide for Applied Research*. San Francisco, CA: Jossey-Bass.

United States General Accounting Office. 2003. *Federal Programs: Ethnographic Studies Can Inform Agencies' Actions*. Washington, DC: US General Accounting Office. Accessed October 1, 2019. https://www.gao.gov/new.items/d03455.pdf.

Wengraf, Tom. 2001. *Qualitative Research Interviewing: Biographic Narrative and Semi-Structured Methods*. Thousand Oaks, CA: Sage.

Williams, Samantha P., Jennine Kinsey, Monique G. Carry, Latasha Terry, Joy Wells, and Karen Kroeger. 2019. Get in, get tested, get care: STD services in urban urgent care centers. *Sexually Transmitted Diseases* 46(10): 648–653.

4   Fieldwork

Key learning outcomes

1 Identify who will be on the field team
2 Prepare for issues related to field safety
3 Conduct effective team debriefings
4 Understand ethical considerations
5 Anticipate potential challenges and solutions

In this chapter, we discuss core elements of planning and carrying out team-based fieldwork. Specifically, we outline important considerations for selecting team members, issues related to field safety, and the various social dynamics embedded in fieldwork. We also provide a framework for understanding how REAs can facilitate partnerships and collaboration with communities, lead to the development of co-learning and skills development opportunities, and enhance the potential for building community-driven research and assessment capacity. Further, we delve into ethics related to community-driven research and common challenges associated with team-based fieldwork.

Fieldwork and field team

Anthropologists define "fieldwork" as "the process of interacting and gathering information at the site or sites where a culture-sharing group is studied" (Beebe 2001). In our work, we define culture as shared beliefs, practices, and values. Most people think of culture as it relates to language, ethnicity, or religion. However, organizations, institutions, and disciplines also have cultures. Whether conscious of them or not, individuals and groups working within these institutions often share beliefs, practices, and values that affect the way priorities are set, resources are used, and how, to whom, and under what conditions services are delivered. For example, our REA work on congenital syphilis highlighted the cultural values of hospital emergency rooms, where physicians described being reluctant to incorporate sexually transmitted disease (STD) testing in these settings due to time constraints—that STD testing could negatively impact the time available to address life-threatening emergencies. In REAs, interviewing people about their work often reveals beliefs and values that need to be articulated and understood in order to make changes.

Who will be on the field team: Skills and characteristics

As in any research project, REA requires careful planning to ensure that work conducted in the field is productive and results in the collection of useful data. This encompasses decisions about who should be interviewed, how and where interviews and observations are carried out, how data are collected and secured, and how the team interacts with community members.

Because teamwork is fundamental to REA, planning also encompasses thoughtful decisions about what will comprise an effective and productive team. This includes who should be on the field team, what type of expertise they should have, and what role or roles they should play in the process. REAs are often intense, with long days of data collection followed by team debriefings, and hours spent expanding and writing up interviews and field notes. Although not everyone is naturally suited to be part of the REA team, most people can be trained to carry out necessary tasks. The best teams are multidisciplinary in nature, comprised of individuals with complementary skill sets and technical or content expertise. In addition, the interpersonal skills and characteristics of potential team members matter a great deal, as the success of the REA will depend to a large degree on how well the team works together to achieve the goals of the project.

Three essential elements of a solid REA team are (1) qualitative methods expertise, (2) content or topical expertise, and (3) cultural expertise. Although the size and scope of REAs vary, when building a team, REA planners should always try to incorporate these three elements.

First, there should be at least one person on the project team with expertise in qualitative research methods, including developing instruments for qualitative interviews, conducting interviews and ethnographic observations, and analysis. Ideally, this should be a person with a background in the social sciences, preferably someone with training in anthropology or ethnography. As mentioned earlier, an ethnographic orientation and sensibility to the project means that the team focuses on learning from participants instead of merely extracting information from them. Rather than passive subjects under study, individuals being interviewed become active participants in the research, sharing their knowledge and expertise with researchers. A person trained in ethnography can help keep the project oriented and on track by monitoring interviews for quality and coaching team members when needed. This person can also elicit information during team debriefings about what is being learned, whether some topics have achieved saturation, the point at which no more new information is being learned, and what threads of information need follow-up.

Second, the team needs individuals with content expertise or relatively deep knowledge of the topic area. Content experts serve several functions. Although all team members should have a basic level of knowledge about the topic, content experts help the overall team navigate through technical aspects and understand the information that is being conveyed by participants. Content experts can be extremely valuable in helping other members of the team understand nuances in process, procedures, or terminology. In our work with state-level STD programs, for example, it was ideal to include a former STD program disease investigator who was familiar with STD surveillance and standard STD program protocols. Team members with content expertise can often interact at a more engaged level with other experts than a novice can and can cover sections of the interview that are more technical in nature, or that need more precise probing than someone without expertise can accomplish. At the same time, content experts are part of a team, and their skills must complement those of other team members. They should not act as authorities and must remain open and non-judgmental during interviews and observations. They should never intimidate or try to sway participants, even if they disagree with what is being said.

Third, the team should, whenever feasible, include "insiders," people with close experience with the problem or phenomenon under study. These are often individuals from the local community or from the population under study. Sometimes these persons are referred to as "cultural experts" (Trotter et al. 2001). In a REA to assess the needs of female sex workers, for example, the "insider" could be a former sex worker, or an outreach worker who has worked closely with the population and is knowledgeable about it. Ideally, a "cultural expert" will be a trusted individual who can help facilitate access to and engagement with hard-to-reach populations, as well as provide insight into how things are organized. A "cultural expert" often has knowledge of local hangouts and is acquainted with gatekeepers that REA teams are unlikely to be able to meet on their own.

Another reason for including "insiders" is that the REA can be a vehicle for transferring research and assessment skills to the local community. By including members of the local population or community, the REA becomes a process for mutual learning and collaboration. The best REAs are those that build meaningful relationships between researchers and researched, a mutually-beneficial collaboration in which participants from the target population are actively engaged in the research. Participants share information with researchers, but in turn, they also reap benefits from the REA. These benefits can be in the form of training in basic research skills which can increase opportunities for other types of employment. REAs can also be catalysts for community change. Including individuals who are part of the community and are affected by the problem is good ethical practice, given that the local community should see some benefit from the project.

REAs are meant to be collaborative exercises, and we encourage REA teams to draw on local expertise whenever possible. In a multi-sited REA in a low-resource country, we were able to identify local academics at a medical school with qualitative research experience. These individuals helped train interviewers and participated in the data analysis. In return, they received training in using software, a skill they were eager to obtain. Local community-based organizations often have talented individuals who are enthusiastic about learning new methods and programs; despite lack of formal university-level training, their hands-on, practical experience with REA may turn them into "experts," enabling them to use these skills for future projects. In summary, if the overall team includes a combination of methods, content, and cultural expertise, the REA has a higher likelihood of success.

There is a fourth cross-cutting element that should be given careful consideration when building the REA team: the interpersonal skills and characteristics of potential team members. As mentioned in the previous chapter on interviewing, team members must be able to establish meaningful engagement with participants and to interact with them in a non-judgmental and respectful manner. Some individuals may have a difficult time considering participants with less traditionally technical skills as experts or may not value indigenous knowledge. Other individuals may find it challenging to work with populations that are engaged in criminalized or stigmatized behaviors due to their own religious, moral, or professional values. Yet others may be fearful of working in neighborhoods or areas that are unfamiliar to them. These individuals may not be well suited to some REAs.

The most important characteristic of an individual is the ability to be a team player. Teams offer the potential to achieve more than any individual could achieve working alone; yet, teams can also be fraught with challenges that can inhibit them from utilizing their diverse set of backgrounds, knowledge, skills, and abilities to perform as well as they could (Mao and Woolley 2016). Team members must be able to work together, complementing each other's strengths and weaknesses to create a cohesive unit. This includes acknowledging and appreciating working with others who come from different social or professional backgrounds. Recognizing each other's knowledge, opinions, and expertise can enhance a team's ability to utilize knowledge and share information more effectively. Teams also benefit from engaging in inclusive behaviors, such as actively eliciting information from other team members and showing appreciation for each other's contributions.

Further, REAs are fast paced due to their time constraints, and schedules often change quickly as new informants and locations are identified within a given field site. Team members must be adaptable, flexible, and able to maintain focus and motivation despite rapidly changing field conditions. At different times, any team member may be interviewer, note taker, observer, navigator, logistician, or driver and should be willing and able to handle any of these tasks without complaint. Individuals who are inflexible, unsettled by working in teams, have poor interdisciplinary and multicultural skills, and are easily frustrated when conditions change are not suitable for REA, even if they possess substantial content expertise. In our work, we sometimes meet people who are under the mistaken impression that the work of being on the REA team begins and ends with conducting interviews. On the contrary, REA team members are expected to contribute to all aspects of the project. Depending on the project, this can entail conducting not only individual in-depth interviews, but also focus groups and street intercept interviews. In addition, it includes carrying out ethnographic observations, generating field notes, actively participating in daily debriefing sessions, assisting with analysis, and writing and commenting on drafts of reports.

Finally, not everyone is comfortable with the approach and limitations inherent in rapid qualitative research. REAs may seem "messy" and lacking rigor to individuals who are highly quantitatively oriented. This is not to say that only people with qualitative training should be on the team; on the contrary, some of the best work we have seen has come from individuals with training in epidemiology, medicine, psychology, and other fields where reliance on quantitative methods is the norm. However, discussion of all of these aspects should occur prior to fieldwork to ensure that the person is a good fit. In our work, we have personally witnessed how poorly-suited team members can alienate participants, create a negative atmosphere, and undermine the goals of the project. The bottom line is that the REA team is greater than the sum of its parts. Teamwork is essential, and as with any such work, if one person fails to carry their load, it can adversely affect the entire project (see Figure 4.1).

Field team size

Although views on the size of REA teams vary, there is general agreement that, when working in one site, teams of four to eight people is most efficient. In our work with state-level programs, we often carried out REAs with

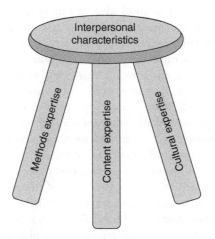

Figure 4.1 A strong REA team: A three-legged stool.

one four-person team over five days. These four individuals usually worked together on planning the assessment, developing the interview guides, securing necessary approvals, conducting the fieldwork, and performing the data analysis and write up. During fieldwork, interviews were usually conducted in pairs of two, with one person conducting the interview and one person recording handwritten notes. This configuration worked well for many of our projects. In a given week, using this plan, we were generally able to carry out 30–35 interviews.

That said, REA projects can vary in size and scope, from small, one-team REAs working in one site over a period of several days, to larger, multi-site projects with multiple REA teams simultaneously collecting data in several cities or locations. At times it may be useful to collect data in additional locations or from different populations of interest in order to make comparisons. Regardless of size, it is important to keep in mind the fundamental principles of REA—that findings be timely, relevant, and able to be used for practical purposes. REA planners should ask: What is the minimum amount of data we need, based on variables of interest, that will give us enough information to be useful, in the time frame that we need it? In general, in our assessments, a pair of REA team members could carry out three to four interviews per day with interviews lasting about an hour on average. Although it would be possible to squeeze in more interviews, this is not ideal because interviewing takes substantial energy. After several interviews, an interviewer wearies and begins to lose focus. In addition, time must be allotted for team travel to interview locations, collecting observations, debriefing, and expanding field notes.

Key factors to consider when determining the size of the REA team include the assessment question, geospatial considerations, infrastructure, logistics, available resources, and the availability of participants. Planners need to take into consideration travel time and costs, the need to work closely with data collection team members, and field safety. Although adding more sites and interviews may seem like a good idea, planners need to consider whether it will be feasible to manage a large and geographically-dispersed team of data collectors and still maintain the quality of interviews and data in what becomes, essentially, a multi-level project. Thought needs to be given to who will lead each team, and how the teams will be structured and deployed into the field. Not least, decisions need to be made about how teams will be expected to debrief, share what they are learning, and make decisions about the overall project. Will dispersed teams be able to debrief together, and have an opportunity to communicate about what is being learned? At times debriefing can be handled through conference calls and remote meetings; however, in low-resourced settings, this may not be feasible. Another aspect to consider when expanding the scope of the project is whether there is enough local research capacity, in terms of qualified staff, to actually carry out the work, and whether this additional burden is feasible and appropriate.

We do not mean to discourage anyone from planning and carrying out large REAs. It is certainly possible—with the right training, planning, and support—to carry out REA in multiple sites at one time, and numerous large and very productive REAs have been conducted over the years. However, large REAs run the risk of becoming overly complex, weighed down by coordination problems and bureaucratic hurdles. Decisions about the parameters of the REA should come about through discussion with the program and its stakeholders. And, as always, decisions about expanding the scope or size of the REA should be based on the need for good data and the ability to manage and, ultimately, use it.

Field team roles and functions

Regardless of whether the REA is carried out by a single team or by multiple teams, there are key roles and functions that need to be assigned to accomplish the overall project. At a minimum, three key roles include the Project Lead, Team Lead, and Field Coordinator. In addition, other REA team members may round out the team, mainly performing data collection and analysis tasks.

The *Project Lead* is responsible for guiding the overall process, and for overseeing any approvals and funding requirements. This person ensures that team members are selected based on REA criteria and that teams are trained. This person often conducts or leads meetings with stakeholders, along with any in-briefings and out-briefings that need to occur in field sites.

The *Team Lead* is responsible for guiding the activities of one REA team in the field and monitoring data collection, including how many interviews and observations have been conducted and ensuring that ethical practices are adhered to by all involved. The REA Team Lead collaborates with fellow team members to carry out the work and may assign interviews and observations to particular team members based on content expertise or other factors. The REA Team Lead communicates with the Project Lead about the project and makes implementation decisions when appropriate. The Team Lead also leads team debriefings. Depending on the size of the project, the same person may carry out both the roles of Project Lead and Team Lead.

As described in the chapter on planning, having an individual with training and experience in ethnography and social science research methods in one or both of these roles is strongly recommended. Although this person may not necessarily be an anthropologist, they will need the skills and expertise to select and train team members in the core ethnographic methods of REA. They will also be called upon to communicate the goals and objectives of the project to stakeholders. This person must be able to convince audiences who may be unfamiliar with the method about the value and benefits of the REA approach. This means explaining the methods and conveying, in persuasive terms, what will be gained by using rapid, qualitative, community-driven, and participatory methods and orientation as opposed to quantitatively-focused work.

Each REA will need a designated *Field Coordinator* who takes the lead on fieldwork logistics and mapping. Logistical planning is an important aspect of REAs. Aspects such as flights, ground transportation, and hotel accommodations, along with initial key interview participants and locations, should be finalized before arrival in the field site. The Field Coordinator's primary functional role is to set up and manage the fieldwork calendar, which includes blocks of time for interviews, observations, and team debriefings. Due to the compressed time schedules of many REAs, team members often have to work quickly to conduct a large number of interviews and observations in a short amount of time. Local collaborators can help orient the REA team by advising on key locations, routes, and other relevant logistics during planning, so that interview and observation schedules can be determined in advance, and time in the field is used efficiently. Waiting until arrival in the field to look around for key informants and observational sites will waste precious time.

However, the team also needs to be flexible. During the continuous debriefings and follow-up during fieldwork, the need for additional interviews or field observations may arise, and the schedule should include built-in time for these changes. Setting up appointments prior to entering the field saves time; however, blocks of time should be left open for interviews and other activities that may emerge as relevant during the course of fieldwork. The Field Coordinator schedules interviews to allow for transportation time between sites and prepares a preliminary schedule to share with the team, knowing that this schedule may change. It is also common to schedule in-brief and out-brief meetings with program officials. These brief meetings can provide local programs an overview of the schedule for fieldwork and an opportunity to share preliminary observations at the end.

REA *team members* perform data collection tasks including interviewing and observing, writing and expanding field notes, and taking part in debriefing sessions. Upon return from the field, team members may be involved in data analysis, writing up the report, and presenting findings.

Debriefing

Debriefing is the process through which team members meet regularly during fieldwork to share what they are learning and to determine the direction of subsequent data collection. Debriefings are a key component of REAs, and time should be built into the schedule so that they are not overlooked. Ideally, debriefings take place at least once a day, but in a compressed REA, this is not always feasible. At a minimum, we recommend teams debrief once every other day while field work is going on.

Debriefings help facilitate teamwork and the spirit of collaborative thinking because they create space for the team to share various perspectives. Information is triangulated across team members, data sources, and data collection methods. Discussion of what has been learned so far serves as a way to identify new topics and emerging themes for follow-up. During debriefings, teams identify areas of inquiry that may need additional probing, as well as those that may have achieved saturation, when no new information about an aspect is being discovered. Teams work together to identify other potential interview participants or contexts to observe and adjust plans for subsequent data collection. Notes should be taken during debriefing sessions to track topics and new lines of inquiry.

In debriefing sessions, teams also discuss progress in the overall project and address any logistical or scheduling problems that have emerged. Debriefing sessions provide time for members to ask questions about methods, obtain coaching and advice, and clarify technical information. Our REAs were often learning experiences for those in research training roles or community members. In such contexts, we encourage team members to switch roles and take on new tasks so that they learn a variety of skills. Debriefing offers a time to ask questions and hone skills. In addition, debriefings are an opportunity for teams to share any concerns they have about safety, logistics, or other fieldwork-related issues.

It is often tempting, due to time constraints, to skip debriefings or to think that matters can be discussed after return from the field, but this is wrong. The process of sharing information and insights in a group setting often makes for a better final report. We recommend building blocks of time into the schedule ahead of time to protect debriefing time. To conclude, debriefing is a critical process that creates opportunities for thinking through and collectively discussing both challenges and opportunities team members face, builds meaningful interpersonal relationships between team members, and facilitates synthesis between collected data and broader contextual issues (see Box 4.1).

Box 4.1

Sample debriefing questions

- Were there any safety issues?
- Were there any unexpected or stressful events?
- How well do you feel you did as an interviewer/note taker? As an observer?
- What type of data did you collect? (e.g., interviews, focus groups, etc.)
- What did you see or hear?
- What things did you learn that were new? Are you still learning new information?
- What things are missing or need to be followed up on?
- Was there anything confirmed?
- What else do we still need to ask?
- For each topic in the guide, what things came up repeatedly?
- Was there anyone mentioned as a new contact that we might want to interview? Are there additional sites or contexts that need to be observed?
- Anything else we should know?

Field team safety

Although establishing rapport with participants is important and researchers may, at times, be observers of illicit activities, REA team members should take care not to engage in these happenings. Maintaining a professional boundary helps to protect participants in the research. Some situations to avoid include engaging in substance use with participants, engaging in any monetary exchange other than those specified for research, soliciting or engaging in sexual activities, and offering or providing personal assistance or counseling, including the use of a personal car, phone, office, etc. In these instances, it may be advisable to refer the person to a local resource such as a community-based organization. REAs may take place in locations or neighborhoods where illicit activities occur, or where people are marginalized by poverty or violence. It is incumbent upon REA team members to avoid engaging in activities or practices that may be illicit or that may endanger themselves, other members of the team, or participants.

One reason our REA teams worked in pairs is for safety. Observing and interviewing in teams is safer than going into some areas as an unaccompanied individual. Other ways to promote safety during fieldwork are to work with the local community-based organizations and leaders prior to beginning fieldwork. Explain the research and its potential benefits so that people are aware that the research will be taking place. Collect background information on the field site before starting work, and if possible, travel into the area with someone who is locally known and trusted until community members are familiar with you. Team members should be clear with people about their role and be wary of manipulation or harassment. Boundaries with participants should be maintained; this means not sharing drugs or having sex with them. If the situation becomes uncomfortable, team members should leave and seek safety. A fellow team member should never be left alone and unattended.

When working in the field, team members need to be alert to their surroundings and anticipate any potential challenges. They should carry official identification, such as a program or agency card. Dressing appropriately for the context is also an important consideration. In most of our work with state programs, we wore casual but professional wear. For some interviews, such as with high school students, jeans were appropriate. Clothing needs to be comfortable and not considered provocative or revealing, or at times, too formal. In some instances, it may be necessary to wear clothing that protects the team member from hazardous materials such as dirty needles or toxic substances. At all times, expensive jewelry and valuables should be left at home.

In addition to physical safety, REA leads and team members need to be aware of the effects of stress and emotional trauma on team members. No matter where it takes place, the intensity and disorientation inherent in fieldwork can be quite stressful to many people. REAs are often physically and mentally exhausting due to the pressure to capture a lot of information in a short amount of time. Interviewing requires enormous focus, which can be draining under the best of circumstances. In addition, fieldwork can take a substantial emotional toll on team members, as they are exposed to unfamiliar, and at times, unpleasant experiences. Some individuals may feel uncomfortable or afraid when entering environments such as drug houses, gay bars, or other places they do not normally frequent. Witnessing the dire poverty in which many people live may be shocking or disturbing. And hours of listening to participants share painful experiences of violence, abuse, or neglect can be emotionally upsetting or deeply depressing to team members. Further, some may find it discomforting to work with others in intimate prolonged contexts (e.g., working together for 10–16 hours a day for 5–7 days). Project leaders need to prepare team members as much as possible for some of these situations and should also try to build time into the schedule for team members to rest, reflect, and re-energize.

Ethics

At all times during fieldwork, REA team members are expected to conduct themselves in an ethical and professional manner. As we discussed in Chapter 2, REAs require the appropriate human subjects protections and approvals and consents before proceeding. Ethical principles for fieldwork are based on protecting participants from any harm the REA could directly or indirectly cause, making sure that participants understand any potential risks and benefits to their participation, and by REA team members maintaining professional boundaries at all times.

REA team members are obligated to assure that the burdens and benefits of research remain equitable and fair among the population groups likely to benefit from research. It is important, therefore, to carefully consider the risks and benefits associated with the research and to continually monitor the research. A critical way to contribute to the safety of research participants is to obtain informed consent. This is most often done in writing (although verbal or oral consent is preferable in certain situations; for example, when a signature might identify someone involved in an illicit activity). Each participant's decision to participate must be voluntary and not coerced. A participant must also be lucid and competent enough to participate and should understand what they have agreed to do by participating. Participants should also be made aware that some questions may carry with them some level of harm of stigma or stress because of the nature of the question. For participants involved in potentially stigmatizing or criminalized behaviors, this may be especially important, although this also applies to individuals who may be discussing their work and talking about supervision or management.

Some REAs will involve investigation into sensitive issues such as sexuality or substance use and abuse, and some individuals may wish to conceal their behavior and identity. Such circumstances require that team members take protective measures to ensure confidentiality and anonymity before, during, and after the research process. It is crucial to avoid collecting participants' names or any other identifying information, and to not share data analyses or findings with anyone outside of the study. Failure to adhere to this has the potential to harm participants and compromises the integrity of the study itself. Data management procedures also need to protect anonymity and confidentiality. This includes protecting data from harmful, outside, or unauthorized access and use; keeping field and observational notes with you at all times; and safely storing and disposing of data and notes.

Potential challenges and solutions

Many of the potential challenges and solutions that occur during fieldwork have been discussed throughout this chapter. Table 4.1 highlights some common scenarios and potential solutions that we have used in our own work on REAs.

Table 4.1 Potential challenges and solutions during fieldwork

Challenge	Solution
A team member often dominates the conversation during debriefing sessions.	Emphasize the importance of teamwork when training field team members. Foster an environment where team members take turns sharing information. Consider having different team members act as facilitators for debriefing sessions and ensure that one person does not dominate. Encourage each team member to participate and share their views.
A team member fails to take part in scheduled debriefings.	During training, emphasize that the success of the REA depends on the team as a whole. Debriefings are a core activity of REA and all team members are expected to take part. Without everyone's contributions, important information or insights may be missed. Although missing a debriefing due to unforeseen circumstances may occur, team members who frequently miss debriefing sessions without good reason may be asked to leave the team.
A team member confides that they are not comfortable with illicit activities they observe.	During training there should be frank and open discussion of the topic and the activities that team members may observe. Team members must be able to be non-judgmental interviewers and observers. Some potential team members may not be suited for certain projects due to personal opinions, religious beliefs, or other values. If this emerges during fieldwork, try to assign less sensitive or stressful tasks to the team member if possible.
Some team members are quantitatively trained and oriented and are unfamiliar with REA or qualitative methods.	Ensure that all team members are trained in interviewing and observational techniques and the basic principles of REA. Be specific about interview, observational, and note-taking protocols. Coach them through the process and provide opportunities for them to fill different roles and tasks. Remind them that the success of REA is based on an interdisciplinary team effort.

Box 4.2

Summary

- Putting together an effective and productive REA field team is critical to its success.
- REA field teams should have a combination of methods, content, and cultural expertise. All members must be team players.
- The size of the field team is dependent on the assessment question, geospatial considerations, infrastructure, logistics, available resources, and member availability.
- Key team members include Project and Team Leads and the Field Coordinator.
- Debriefing is a fundamental aspect of team-based fieldwork where team members meet to discuss what they are learning and the direction of subsequent data collection.
- Safety and ethical issues should be considered throughout the fieldwork period.

References

Beebe, James. 2001. *Rapid Assessment Process: An Introduction*. Walnut Creek, CA: Altamira Press.

Mao, Anna T., and Anita Williams Woolley. 2016. Teamwork in health care: Maximizing collective intelligence via inclusive collaboration and open communication. *AMA Journal of Ethics* 18(9): 933–940.

Trotter, Robert T., Richard H. Needle, Eric Goosby, Christopher Bates, and Merrill Singer. 2001. A methodological model for rapid assessment, response and evaluation: The RARE program in public health. *Field Methods* 13(2): 137–159.

5 Data analysis

Key learning outcomes

1 Identify principles of REA team-based, collaborative analysis
2 Develop strategies for building an effective analysis team
3 Define the steps in the analysis cycle
4 Characterize practices for managing and reducing data
5 Describe techniques used in rapid analysis
6 Anticipate potential challenges and solutions

In this chapter, we provide an overview of the critical elements of team-based, collaborative analysis. We clarify how to build an analytical team within REAs, and how to involve and train community members in data analysis procedures and generating preliminary findings. We also discuss the essential aspects of qualitative data management and analysis, as well as the principles of triangulation. Finally, we consider key issues related to rapid, team-based data analysis including developing analytical aims and objectives, working with different analytical styles, managing data, attending to issues of reliability and validity, and working with computer-based qualitative analysis software.

There are excellent materials available on ethnographic and qualitative data analysis and it is impossible and impractical to cover all of the various approaches here. In this chapter, we will provide a basic overview of qualitative data analysis and focus on key principles and techniques related to REA. We concentrate on strategies and practices that will enable data analysis to be conducted quickly and efficiently, while at the same time facilitating collaboration with local communities and populations to strengthen the validity of findings and increase the likelihood that the final report and recommendations have value.

Analysis team

REA teams, by design, are comprised of individuals from different disciplines or professional backgrounds, along with community members who may have various levels of education and no formal research training at all.

This allows for diverse perspectives on a problem, but it can also create a challenge when it comes to conducting analysis. It is important, therefore, that the REA data analysis processes be cooperative, understandable, engaging, and inclusive of community researchers. As emphasized in earlier chapters, someone on the team, preferably the project or team lead, needs to be experienced in conducting qualitative data analysis. This person's role is to manage the process and guide the team. This person may help to structure and shape the analysis to fit the goals of the project, while at the same time ensuring that the analysis process remains team-based and collaborative. This does not mean that every member of the data collection team will be hands on in the nitty-gritty of coding data, but it does mean that they are involved at various stages and provide input and reflection on how the data are interpreted. In the sections below we will describe some approaches we have used in our REA projects.

Qualitative data management and preparation

Timely data analysis depends on successful data management. Data management practices should be outlined concretely before beginning the REA. First, team members should account for the variety of data sources: these could include audio files, handwritten or typed field notes, prepared transcripts, map drawings, and photographs, among others. The team should think about how the data will be analyzed or used, and not collect more data than is necessary to meet the goals of the project. Too many projects seem to collect data for the sake of collecting it without a clear purpose, "just in case" it might be interesting or useful down the road. In REAs, which are meant to be timely and practical, the focus should be on usable data.

Data management requires developing systems and protocols for recording data, keeping track of materials, and storing or transferring them. Before conducting the REA, the team should develop a clear organization system for qualitative and ethnographic data, and each member should be trained in established protocols for preparing field notes, transcripts, maps, and other materials. There is nothing more disappointing than realizing (at the end of fieldwork, no less!) that one team member has been jotting down a few bullet points rather than taking verbatim notes because they were inadequately trained or prepared, or there was not a clear protocol for note-taking. When preparing interview transcripts, for example, whether from notes or from recordings, the end product should be formatted according to an agreed-upon protocol—including labeling, dating, and numbering of interviews; font and font size; margins; and conventions for how to take account of contextual data such as pauses or silences.

The team should create a data organization file or log that includes dates, locations, defining individual and group participant characteristics, interviewer identification, and other important features, including naming conventions for original data files and subsequent analysis. In our REAs, we created an Excel spreadsheet with this information, and updated it as interview transcripts and other materials were added to the project. Logs were routinely cross-checked with the interview schedule to ensure that all interviews were accounted for.

All data, particularly digital recordings of interviews or visual materials (e.g., photographs, maps, etc.) should be thoroughly reviewed to ensure fidelity of analyzed data to original conversations and observations. If ethics agreements require that no names or identifying characteristics be recorded, all identifying information must be removed from final transcripts before analysis begins. If data are collected and stored on smartphones or other devices and analyzed by using qualitative data analysis (QDA) software, maintaining careful control over the data files is important, especially when multiple analysts are involved. This standardization saves time during analysis, prevents valuable data from being lost, and helps facilitate both manual and computer assisted coding.

Using software

It is possible to conduct analysis of REA data by hand, using rapid methods for extracting and coding data. In cases where there are few resources or a lack of technical training, this might be necessary. Thirty years ago, analysis was often conducted by hand, using color-coded highlighters and other methods, or simple word processing programs to capture data. Today, however, most REA data sets are organized and analyzed with the aid of QDA software programs such as Atlas.ti and NVivo that help manage and reduce the large amounts of text that result from in-depth interviews, focus groups, and observations. New programs are being developed at a rapid pace and a review of these is beyond the scope of this book. Many of these software programs have regular, commercial, or trial subscriptions, and offer a variety of remote and in-person webinars, workshops, and demonstrations, some for free.

QDA programs are useful in automating steps in the analysis, running queries and reports, and helping to maintain quality control. Having someone on the team who is proficient in the use of a QDA software program will undoubtedly speed up the process of analysis. However, we cannot emphasize enough that QDA programs do not "do" analysis. Each interview transcript still requires the labor-intensive work of reading, reflecting, reviewing, and coding. And some QDA programs can be expensive. Decisions about whether to use software, which program to use, and who should lead or guide the analysis should be part of the initial planning process and factored into the overall budget. In many projects, purchasing software and training or mentoring local staff are opportunities for transferring skills and engaging community members in the analysis, which can help justify the added cost of software.

Qualitative data analysis

Ideally, in all qualitative and ethnographic projects, analysis occurs in tandem with data collection and continues until results are reported out. The concept of saturation presumes that data are being reviewed and reflected upon as data collection is being conducted. The direction of data collection may change depending on what new information is being learned and what needs follow up. Saturation occurs when data collection yields no more new information. Although data are not yet being formally coded, they are continually being thought about and reflected upon. According to Seidel (1998), data analysis is an iterative and cyclical process of noticing, collecting, and thinking about information you've seen and heard (see Figure 5.1). In noticing, team members pay attention to what is going on using observations, notes, and interviews, reading through field notes, and participating in team debriefings. In collecting, they begin to organize things that group together such as facts, categories, concepts, and themes. In thinking, the analysis team looks for patterns and relationships in the data in order to develop conclusions and recommendations (see Box 5.1).

This is also true for REA, as team members expand field notes and debrief together on a regular basis in the field. The analysis process continues as the team begins to work more closely with transcripts and other data by reading, writing memos, and coding text. REA analysis is always team-based and

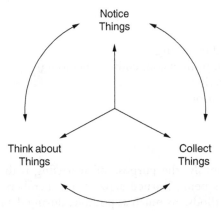

Figure 5.1 Qualitative data analysis: An iterative process.

Seidel, John V. 1998. *Qualitative Data Analysis.* Colorado Springs, CO: Qualis Research. Accessed October 1, 2019, http://www.qualisresearch.com/DownLoads/qda.pdf

---

Box 5.1

Data analysis: An iterative process

- Noticing

    o Paying attention to what is going on
    o Observations, notes, interviews
    o Field notes and team debriefings

- Collecting

    o Organizing things that group together
    o Facts, categories, concepts, themes

- Thinking

    o Looking for patterns and relationships in the data
    o Developing conclusions and recommendations

(Seidel 1998)

---

iterative, beginning in the field and continuing until the final report is completed and disseminated (see Figure 5.2).

Components of analysis

Analysis can sometimes seem daunting, mostly because it is difficult to determine where and how to begin. To make analysis a less intimidating process, we break it down into four key components:

1 Debriefing and memoing
2 Data reduction (immersion, coding, memoing)
3 Data interpretation
4 Data representation

Debriefing

As discussed previously, the purpose of debriefing is to communicate and triangulate what is being learned across team members, data sources, and data collection methods. As much as possible, during debriefings REA team members should avoid preconceived ideas about the way things are or should be, and instead focus specifically on what is being seen and heard. It is important to talk and process this information before relating it to explanations you already know about or assign meaning and make interpretations too soon. Debriefing sessions are part of data collection and analysis and notes

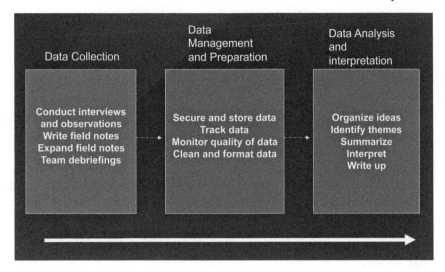

Figure 5.2 Analysis process tasks.

from debriefing meetings should be documented using summary write-ups, matrices, or maps. Debriefing sessions are also points where the REA team should make decisions about subsequent data collection including issues related to theoretical saturation and triangulation.

Memoing

Memoing is another important aspect of analysis. Memoing is the process of writing reflective notes about the data. Memoing can be done to write down thoughts on preliminary speculation, theory, and other related issues. It can also reflect ideas and insights that help with data interpretation, meaning, and context as well as explanations for patterns and themes identified through the analysis.

Memoing can be used at different stages in the analysis process—during data collection to reflect on interviews and observations as they are being conducted, but also after return from the field as part of data reduction and analysis. In some of our projects, team members wrote memos about each interview or observational field notes to jot down ideas and thoughts about possible interpretation. In another project, we used memos later in the analysis process. Text was coded and the team reviewed all of the text captured within codes and wrote memos to help summarize and capture the main points in coded content. We started with a relatively small codebook and "chunked" larger amounts of data together, and then wrote memos on the larger chunks, which were shared among the analysis team. The team then met together and used memos to make determinations and consensus decisions about developing additional codes (or sub-codes) and conducted more granular coding to capture ideas and potential themes identified in the memos. This process also helped us think about the priorities for subsequent analysis and about the overall structure of the report.

Data reduction

After data have been cleaned, managed, and stored, the analysis team embarks on the process of "selecting, focusing, simplifying, abstracting, and trans-forming" data (Miles and Huberman 1994:10). During this phase, informa-tion is broken down in a multi-step process. This includes getting a sense of the data holistically (i.e., immersion), categorizing data into groupings and clusters to make meaning of that data (i.e., coding), and writing reflective notes about data (i.e., memoing), all while retaining the context in which data occur (see Box 5.2). Data reduction can be done manually or by using QDA software. This phase will be the most time-consuming aspect of the data analysis.

Immersion

Much of qualitative analysis consists of careful, methodical, and contin-ual reading of text and other visual material to identify how bits of data hold together and how themes and interconnections emerge from the data. Repeatedly reading and viewing these materials helps analysts identify themes, associations between themes, and complexities and contradictions in the text, yielding deeper meanings than if one were to read just once or in a cursory manner. In REAs, field notes and interview transcripts are writ-ten collaboratively. Reading full texts of field notes and transcripts multiple times, then, offers analysts a way to understand the broader context of what is happening in field sites and interviews before breaking up text into codes and themes for separate analysis.

Box 5.2

Data reduction

"Data reduction is not something separate from analysis. It is part of analysis. The researcher's decisions—which data chunks to code and which to pull out, which evolving story to tell—are all analytic choices. Data reduction is a form of analysis that sharpens, sorts, focuses, discards, and organizes data in such a way that 'final' conclusions can be drawn and verified."

(Miles and Huberman 1994:11)

Coding

Coding is a systematic way to condense large amounts of text into smaller analyzable units through a system of labeling and then sorting them into concepts and categories. Coding eventually enables analysts to identify overall themes in the data and to explore patterns and relationships among different ideas and themes. Concepts are the key ideas or notions that relate to the research question or questions. In a REA investigating HIV risk, for example, some concepts might be "risk" or "condoms" or "STDs." These concepts are given labels, or codes, that are then used to sort, group, and compare similar bits of text (or segments). Coding begins with team members working together to look at all the data, identifying bits of data that are similar, and putting these bits into common groupings (see Table 5.1). These initial groupings can then be assorted into higher levels (see below in the section on data interpretation). Coding can be done either manually using a variety of inexpensive tools (e.g., colored paper, highlighters, easel pads) or QDA software.

In qualitative projects, it is standard practice to develop a codebook in the early stages of the project that all coders will use and adhere to (see Table 5.2). Codes need to be well-defined with clear definitions and parameters for inclusion and exclusion so that they can be applied in a consistent manner by team members. There is no one way to develop a codebook and apply codes. Some analysts prefer beginning with fewer codes and then expanding the codebook as needed; others prefer starting with more codes and then lumping codes together ("splitters vs. lumpers"). But in general, there should be no more than 20–30 codes when starting out. Codebooks also evolve—as the analysis proceeds, some codes may be dropped and others created, depending on what is needed. The important thing is that codes are applied to text in a consistent manner by all team members. In most instances, teams work together in the early stages of coding to agree upon a set of codes and how they will be applied. This is sometimes accomplished by having multiple team members read the same transcript and make notes about the concepts and ideas they see in the data. The team meets to discuss,

Table 5.1 Example of text-based coding

Text	Code	Memo
They think, "Oh it's just syphilis and I can get a shot to treat it. No big deal."	Syphilis Syphtx	Syphilis is an easy fix.
When you are high as a kite, you don't think, "Oh I need to rip that condom open."	Drugs Condom use	Aware should use a condom but drugs impair judgment or action.
Back then, active HIV testing was a way of showing support for your community.	HIV testing Community support	HIV testing as a moral action. Generational differences between then and now.

Table 5.2 Codebook example

Code	Definition	Example text
Barriers	The participant describes things, structures, or conditions that impede the use of services	"Well, the clinic is only open from 8 until 2 and the test costs $20, so that's a problem for a lot of our clients. Plus, there's still a lot of stigma attached to HIV and STD testing. Some people are ashamed or embarrassed."
Trust	The participant uses the term "trust" or "distrust" (or a synonym) or provides a concrete example of these in what they relate	"The other thing is that people just don't trust the system. They don't see the Health Department as a safe place to come and they worry about confidentiality."

compare, and then agree upon a set of codes that will be used. They then code additional interviews and meet again to make adjustments or changes to the codebook. Throughout the analysis, the team may meet periodically to compare coding, tweak codes, and discuss emerging themes. This is part of an ongoing and iterative process in which the team works together to develop ideas for the report.

Although there is no one way to distribute the work of coding and analyzing data, we have found that, even for small REAs, having no less than two people involved in the mechanics of coding is a productive strategy. This decision is usually made based on the size of the project and the available human and technical resources, including the availability of software; if four people have access to software, they might all code data. Work can be divided in different ways; for example, one person might code all the provider interviews, while another codes all the patient interviews. How the work is distributed depends on the project and the size of the team. Regardless, however, other remaining team members should also be involved. This can be accomplished by having them review coding and write memos, having them write and review sections of the report, or having them be involved in other phases of the analysis. Having multiple team members involved in the analysis ensures that there are multiple perspectives brought to bear and helps ward off tunnel vision in the interpretation of data.

There are different approaches to coding, depending on the researcher and the needs of the project. In REAs, we have found that a dual approach that uses both deductive and inductive coding has been most helpful.

Deductive, sometimes called "a priori" or "top down" coding, is the assignment of text to predetermined categories or codes. Often these codes are *theory-driven,* in which codes are suggested by the research literature, or *question-driven,* in which codes are structured by the interview guide and research question, or the goals of the REA. Inductive, or "bottom up," coding comes directly from ideas or concepts that emerge from reading, thinking, and discussing the data. In REAs, deductive coding has been useful in capturing information to directly respond to research questions or priorities of the project. The codes have often helped to provide a structure for starting out with the data analysis and for making sure that some questions are not overlooked.

Inductive codes have tended to emerge during the analysis when we were working closely with the data. These codes were often related to insights or deeper explanations that were being discovered as the analysis proceeded (see Figure 5.3). Deductive coding can be useful during a "first pass" of the data, when data are being sorted into large chunks. However, caution should be used because this can also result in an inordinate focus on the responses to interview questions or observational field notes rather than seeing the data holistically. Instead, it is preferable to have the team read a subset of interviews or observational field notes and develop a list of codes based on the content of the interviews or observational field notes. This preliminary list of codes can be the basis for the initial codebook. In our REAs we tended to use both these

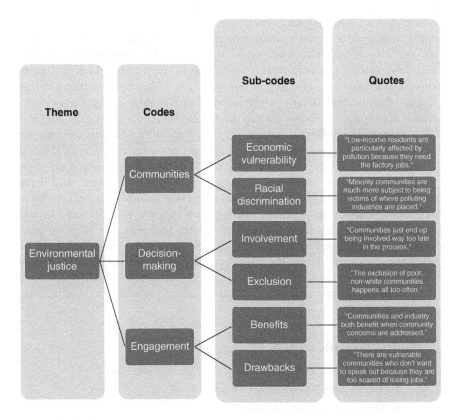

Figure 5.3 Coding process.

Mittmann, Helen, Thurka Sangaramoorthy, and Devon Payne-Sturges. 2017. Social Life of Policy: Cumulative Impact Legislation in Maryland. Poster, Maryland Public Health Association Annual Conference, College Park, MD.

coding strategies, starting with codes based on close reading of interviews and observational field notes, but also generating a set of a priori codes.

Data interpretation (meaning making)

Next, using the codes and any additional notes, analysts can explore the data for emerging themes, patterns, and relationships. Themes are essentially "chunks" of related data or codes that have similar meanings. Those "chunks" then become clustered in similar theme categories. The analysis team then creates meaning for those categories with labels, and the themes emerge from those categories. The team interprets themes to answer the original research questions. These steps will enable analysts to group ideas that are similar and contradictory and to develop provisional descriptions of the findings (see Box 5.3).

Themes, in essence, draw codes together from one or more data sources to present findings from research in a coherent and meaningful way. For instance, in a qualitative study regarding pharmacy practice and patients' perceptions of treatment plans, researchers used codes such as "not being listened to" or "lack of interest in personal experiences" to identify topics, issues, and similarities across participants' narratives of the way in which they were treated in a hospital setting. They brought these codes together into a theme that ran through the narratives which then they labeled as "the patient's experience of hospital care" (Sutton and Austin 2015).

Further, analysts should note any gaps in data or any outliers as these are important parts of data analysis. Once preliminary conclusions are drawn, it is important to explore how these ideas relate and compare to initial observations and interviews. Sometimes, group discussion using imagery and manual tools (e.g., easel pads, sticky notes, dry erase boards) can be helpful in developing themes and connections between themes. Careful analysis and synthesis of data leads to findings that are both representative of participant views and meaningful to readers. Conclusions drawn by researchers must be supported by direct quotations from participants and other data sources, so

---

Box 5.3

Steps to thematic analysis

- Think about information in context: how, when, where, how often
- Categorize relationships among data "bits"
  - o   Things that happen together
  - o   The order things tend to happen
  - o   Things that cause other things
  - o   Things that prevent other things from happening

that it is clear that the themes under discussion have emerged from the data collected and not the researcher's perspective.

Data representation

Portraying information from REA succinctly, efficiently, and with illustrative details is an important aspect of analysis. Decisions regarding how data are summarized and displayed facilitate how findings are received by readers and influence the depth and detail of the final report. Visual displays, in addition to text and narrative, can communicate ideas, relationships, situational dynamics, and other concepts in a qualitative dataset. For instance, matrix tables can compare men and women in terms of themes or categories. Concept models can help lay out complex ideas or relationships graphically for the reader. Tree or hierarchical diagrams can represent levels of analysis. Narrative framework that structures the data chronologically, thematically, or through a focus on critical incidents may be helpful. Visual representation can serve as a great complement to narrative data. Figures, tables, charts, matrices, trees, diagrams, photos, and maps can help convey complicated ideas in a simple, visually engaging way (see Figures 5.4–5.7 and Table 5.3).

Triangulation

Once the REA is completed, there will be multiple data sources such as interview transcripts, observational field notes, focus group recordings, photographs and other visual materials, and mapping diagrams with which to work. Analysts should begin by reflecting on the project's original aims and how different components of data gathered relate to those aims. Triangulation is the use of several sources and methods to substantiate that the information learned from one source and one method converges with another (Carter et al. 2014). This strengthens internal validity as information learned through one source, method, or researcher is compared against what is learned from another (Golafshani 2003). In REA, intensive team interaction helps to increase validity by bringing to bear multiple perspectives and approaches to the problem. This is especially true when teams include local community members or members of the affected population, and not just academically-trained researchers. Triangulation is not so much a method of systematically testing one theory against another as it is an orientation and practice that operates holistically—taking in the big picture—and collaboratively across researchers and community members.

Member checking

The analysis team has an obligation to share the results of their analysis with participants who provided information before the report is finalized. This is sometimes referred to as "member checking" and can be done at different

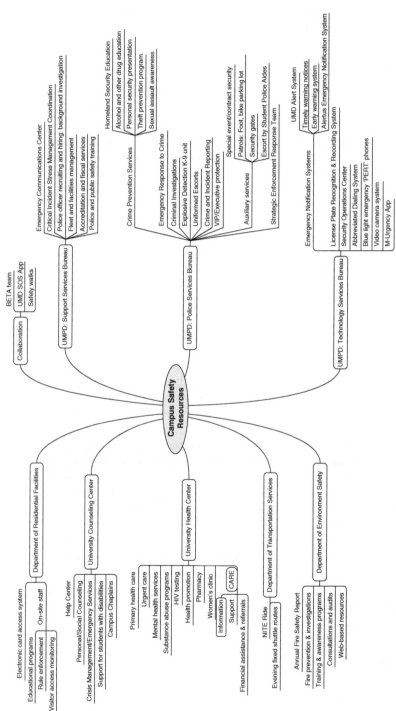

Figure 5.4 Social map of campus safety resources and services.

Students in Sangaramoorthy's qualitative research methods class investigated the perceived availability and effectiveness of campus safety resources for female undergraduate students at the University of Maryland, College Park. Using participant observation, mapping, and interviews, students created this map to visually represent their findings of various campus safety resources that were available to female undergraduate students.

Kearney, Maya, Evelyn Lopez, Stephanie Madden, Janna Napoli, and Soren Peterson. 2013. "Perceived Campus Safety Resources for College Women on the University of Maryland, College Park Campus." ANTH606: Qualitative Methods in Applied Anthropology Final Paper, University of Maryland.

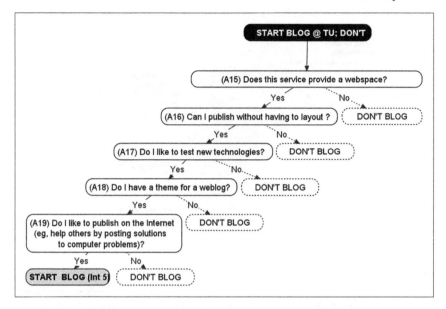

Figure 5.5 Ethnographic decision-tree modeling.

Figure 5.5 shows an example of an individual decision-tree model about whether to start a weblog. The various decision criteria were elicited from the interviews and arranged in the diagrams, following the thoughts of the students. Dotted lines and forms in the figures represent what students mentioned as important factors in the decision-making process, solid lines represent their actual decision-making process. This model can be read as a series of if-then conditions. Can do one for each interview and also do a composite tree.

Andergassen, Monika, Reinhold Behringer, Janet Finlay, Andrea Gorra, and David Moore. 2009. Weblogs in Higher Education – why do Students (not) Blog? *Electronic Journal of e-Learning* 7: 203-215.

intervals, either informally or formally. By design, REAs can never be comprehensive in the sense that they cannot cover every topic to the fullest and most accurate extent. Given the rapidity with which REAs are carried out, some things will inevitably be missed or some nuance will be misunderstood. It is important to give participants a chance to correct facts, weigh in on interpretations, and supplement partial information. This does not mean, however, that the REA team agrees to withhold information because it is perceived as embarrassing or negative or to change the results of the analysis. Member checking should always be presented as an opportunity for participants to help the REA team "get things right." At times this means incorporating perspectives that seem to run counter to the main thesis of the analysis. REAs are not about counting or finding only agreement but should seek to illustrate a range of ideas in perspectives.

When member checking in our work, we sometimes provided summary tables of findings to key informants and asked them to weigh in on them. It is not necessary to check in with everyone who was interviewed, but there

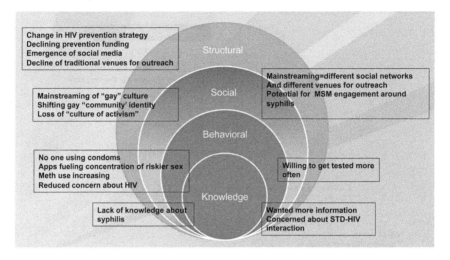

Figure 5.6 Example of figure: Perceptions about syphilis increases among MSM in Portland.

Figure 5.6 illustrates the main themes of an assessment of factors underlying persistent increases in syphilis among MSM in Portland, Oregon. Themes and recommendations were organized according to whether they were related to knowledge, behavioral factors, social factors, or structural factors.

Kroeger, Karen, Melissa Habel, Neetu Abad, Emily Petrosky, Damian Denson, Joanne Castle, Amy Zlot, Michael LaClair, Malini DeSilva, Sean Schafer, and Kim Toevs. 2014. *What Do Gay Men Say about Syphilis? Perceptions of Community Members and Health Care Providers Regarding Syphilis Increases in Portland, Oregon.* Poster presentation, National STD Prevention Conference, Atlanta, GA.

Table 5.3 Data table example: Syphilis symptoms mentioned by MSM

These terms were extracted from interviews with MSM in which they shared their perceptions about signs and symptoms of syphilis. Information was captured during coding, and then organized by category for the report summary. Table 5.3 reflects both accurate knowledge of syphilis symptoms, as well as confusion of syphilis symptoms with those of other STDs. This information enabled public health workers to address specific misperceptions when communicating with MSM about syphilis and other STDs.

Urogenital	*Dermatological*	*Neurological*
Burning urination★	Blisters on genitals★	Brain impairment or damage
Discharge or puss from genitals★	Blisters on mouth★	Hearing loss
Foul odors in genital area★	Hair loss	Dementia
Rotten pee★	Lesions on hands	Stroke
	Lesions on genitals	Vision problems
	Spots on body	
	Body rash	
	Warts★	

★ *Indicates sign or symptom not generally associated with syphilis*

Kroeger, Karen, Melissa Habel, Neetu Abad, Emily Petrosky, Damian Denson, Joanne Castle, Amy Zlot, Michael LaClair, Malini DeSilva, Sean Schafer, and Kim Toevs. 2014. *What Do Gay Men Say about Syphilis? Perceptions of Community Members and Health Care Providers Regarding Syphilis Increases in Portland, Oregon.* Poster presentation, National STD Prevention Conference, Atlanta, GA.

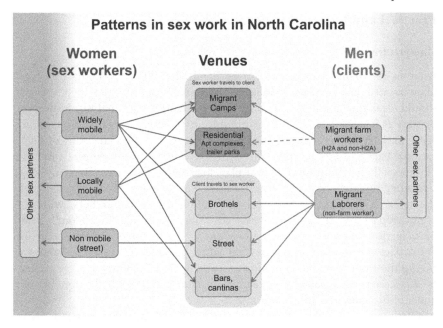

Figure 5.7 Example of concept model: Patterns in sex work in North Carolina.

This model illustrates the "landscape" of sexual risk among migrant Latino men and female sex workers in North Carolina. Figure 5.7 illustrates that contacts between sex workers and clients are not necessarily random, but instead are the result of interactions that are structured by type of sex work and mobility, type of venue, and work status.

Sangaramoorthy, Thurka and Karen Kroeger. 2013. Mobility, Latino migrants, and the geography of sex work: Using ethnography in public health assessments. *Human organization* 72(3): 263–272.

should be an effort made to reach out to some of the participants before the report is finalized. This could mean sharing a draft report with people in the program. It might also mean conducting a presentation at town hall or community meeting where a group of stakeholders can provide feedback on the preliminary findings. It is important to become aware of and correct any serious inaccuracies in data or interpretation before a final report goes out. In some cases, if time and resources allow, member checking may lead to a few additional key informant interviews being conducted to round out an interpretation.

Member checking is a critical part of analysis. It is important to the overall accuracy of the findings and the integrity of the analysis. More importantly, it is another step in the collaborative process of working with a community to find solutions to problems. There is absolutely no point in conducting REA if ultimately the results are viewed as deeply flawed, irrelevant, or not representative of participant perspectives because the recommendations are unlikely to be accepted or implemented.

Practical and logistical issues to consider

Analysis team

Analysis for many assessments can be handled easily with a small analysis team located in one place. Members who are responsible for data analysis should ideally have some experience with qualitative data analysis. However, because REAs often consist of community partners and organizational staff, there may be differences between analysis team members in terms of educational backgrounds and previous experiences with conducting research. It is important to accommodate and plan for these differences. In many participatory research contexts, communities partner with researchers to drive the research agenda, but the analysis is often left to researchers, who are considered to have the analytical expertise (Jackson 2008). We encourage the participation of community members and organizational staff in analyzing REA data beyond member checking when possible. This can be done by taking the time to create an inclusive, team-focused analysis process guided by a researcher (e.g., project or team lead) who is well trained in qualitative and ethnographic research methods.

There are several issues to consider when selecting members of the analysis team. Although it is understood that there may be varying education and literacy levels of the group, individuals may need to have a minimum level of reading and writing skills to participate in analysis, possess positive interpersonal skills that allow them to work in a team-based environment, and be dependable and interested in executing analysis tasks and responsibilities. Although it may take some extra time, the REA project and/or team lead could conduct hands-on training on research analysis. This training should focus on a brief review of REA methods and the project, an orientation to data management and the process of triangulation, and analysis steps. The analysis process needs to be understandable and engaging to non-researchers (Jackson 2008). It is beneficial to break down the process into smaller steps using team-based and small group work using interactive, engaging, and more visual techniques (e.g., color highlighters, sticky notes, easel pads).

Other major considerations to discuss include theoretical approaches to analysis (e.g., phenomenology, hermeneutics, grounded theory), analytical style (e.g., lots of codes vs. few codes, structured vs. unstructured), and use of computers (e.g., e-mail, electronic data vs. paper). An analyst who is accustomed to unstructured coding, for example, may find a highly structured coding scheme difficult to work with, especially if coming into a project at an intermediate phase. These discussions are helpful for understanding how to structure data collection and analysis and where talents and methods can be put to their best use.

Consistent with the team-based and participatory orientation of REAs, the analysis process must be inclusive, facilitating team members' learning, encouraging their participation, and valuing their ideas. The project and team lead and other team members need to be committed to working with community members and organizational staff through the analysis phase rather than taking over the process. Actively listening, checking in, and encouraging insights and ideas from all members can greatly facilitate co-learning and deeper analysis.

Data management and analysis

As the volume of data builds, finding relevant information and managing the different items, such as transcripts, notes, and early ideas becomes more difficult. As we stated previously, it is critical that the REA team, from the outset, develop a clear organizational system for data. We've often found it helpful to conduct analysis in stages or phases to make it less overwhelming. It may also make sense to split up into smaller groups to conduct initial analysis, and then work together as a team to analyze the full data set. Condensing or reducing the data by selecting, focusing, simplifying, and abstracting allows for a more seamless transformation of this condensed data into information that can then be analyzed. Each stage of data management, reduction, and analysis involves multiple decisions that require clear rules and close supervision.

Also, there are potential technical challenges of working across institutions in terms of computer hardware and software. Before embarking on a large multi-site rapid assessment, discuss and think through the logistical challenges of moving or transferring data. Not everyone will have the same equipment or software and power sources may be undependable. Some QDA software may need to include licensing parameters that allow for multiple sites or users to work on one data set, and at times, different computer operating systems (e.g., Mac vs PC). It is helpful, therefore, to think about who will be available to code the data and write the report. Additionally, some team members may need to return to their primary assignments and may have limited availability.

Box 5.4

Summary

- Analysis begins with the first interview and ends when the report is final.
- Analysis in REA is an iterative, team-based process of noticing, collecting, and thinking about things you are seeing and hearing.
- Four components of analysis include debriefing and memoing; data reduction; data interpretation; and data representation.
- Triangulation integrates insights from a variety of data sources, methods, researchers, and interpretations to create a deep understanding of a phenomenon.
- Member checking is an opportunity for participants to help the REA team draw stronger, more meaningful conclusions.

References

Andergassen, Monika, Reinhold Behringer, Janet Finlay, Andrea Gorra, and David Moore. 2009. Weblogs in higher education – Why do students (not) blog? *Electronic Journal of e-Learning* 7(3): 203–215.

Carter, Nancy, Denise Bryant-Lukosius, Alba DiCenso, Jennifer Blythe, and Alan J. Neville. 2014. The use of triangulation in qualitative research. *Oncology Nursing Forum* 41(5): 545–547.

Golafshani, Nahid. 2003. Understanding reliability and validity in qualitative research. *The Qualitative Report* 8(4): 597–606.

Jackson, Suzanne F. 2008. A participatory group process to analyze qualitative data. *Progress in Community Health Partnerships: Research, Education, and Action* 2(2): 161–170.

Kearney, Maya, Evelyn Lopez, Stephanie Madden, Janna Napoli, and Søren Peterson. 2013. "Perceived Campus Safety Resources for College Women on the University of Maryland, College Park Campus." ANTH606: Qualitative Methods in Applied Anthropology Final Paper, University of Maryland.

Kroeger, Karen, Melissa Habel, Neetu Abad, Emily Petrosky, Damian Denson, Joanne Castle, Amy Zlot, Michael LaClair, Malini DeSilva, Sean Schafer, and Kim Toevs. 2014. *What Do Gay Men Say about Syphilis? Perceptions of Community Members and Health Care Providers Regarding Syphilis Increases in Portland, Oregon.* Poster presentation, National STD Prevention Conference, Atlanta, GA.

Miles, Matthew B., and A. Michael Huberman. 1994. *Qualitative Data Analysis: An Expanded Sourcebook.* Thousand Oaks, CA: Sage.

Mittmann, Helen, Thurka Sangaramoorthy, and Devon Payne-Sturges. 2017. Social Life of Policy: Cumulative Impact Legislation in Maryland. Poster, Maryland Public Health Association Annual Conference, College Park, MD.

Sangaramoorthy, Thurka and Karen Kroeger. 2013. Mobility, Latino migrants, and the geography of sex work: Using ethnography in public health assessments. *Human Organization* 72(3): 263–272.

Seidel, John V. 1998. *Qualitative Data Analysis.* Colorado Springs, CO: Qualis Research. Accessed on October 1, 2019. http://www.qualisresearch.com/DownLoads/qda.pdf

Sutton, Jane and Zubin Austin. 2015. Qualitative research: Data collection, analysis, and management. *The Canadian Journal of Hospital Pharmacy* 68(3): 226–231.

6 Report writing and follow up

Key learning outcomes

1 Effectively present key findings and outcomes
2 Write clear, concrete, and actionable recommendations
3 Create a dissemination plan for key findings
4 Develop follow-up plan to address future needs
5 Anticipate potential challenges and solutions

In this chapter, we describe how REA team members develop and communicate results and findings to a variety of recipients such as program administrators and managers, community leaders and members, key decision makers, funders, and policy makers. We provide step-by-step instructions on how to write clear, concrete, and actionable recommendations for different audiences, develop pragmatic dissemination plans for REA findings, and construct strategies for following up after the REA has concluded. We also discuss issues such as data sharing, publishing REA findings, and touch on potential challenges and solutions related to community-driven research based on rapid methods research that may arise during the dissemination phase.

Who are the audiences for the report?

As part of planning for the REA, the team needs to determine the audience(s) for the REA and the types of products that will be needed to communicate the REA team's findings. Often, there will be multiple audiences, and it is important to establish early on which materials the REA team will be responsible for and who will receive these products.

At a minimum, the REA team will likely be responsible for producing a written report that describes the project and its findings, along with any recommendations that stem from the findings. This report is usually delivered to the agency or entity that is funding the REA. In addition to the written report, there may also be a need for presentations to stakeholders and community members, brief summaries aimed at decision makers or legislators, scientific presentations at conferences, and publications for peer-reviewed journals. The REA team may produce some or all of these, depending upon the resources and the agreements made with funders or other key stakeholders.

It is good practice to have a discussion early in the planning process about responsibility for and authorship of any planned reports, publications, and presentations to ensure that expectations and responsibilities are clear and agreed upon from the outset. Will a written report directed at program managers become the basis for a peer-reviewed manuscript for wider publication? If so, who will write and author this manuscript? Will the REA team be expected to create a presentation for a town hall with stakeholders? This is often a negotiation between the REA team responsible for carrying out the work and the agency or entity funding the project. Having all pertinent information regarding products for which the REA team is responsible documented in a brief statement of work will reduce the possibility of misunderstandings or conflict later on.

It is also useful to have a discussion of who will have access to the original data in the form of REA notes, recordings, or transcripts after the REA concludes. Often this is addressed in a formal and approved protocol prior to the start of the REA. Confidentiality agreements with interview participants may stipulate that recordings be destroyed at the end of the project, and that de-identified transcripts will also be destroyed. Individuals accustomed to working with quantitative data may express interest in having access to REA data after the project is over. However, data use and sharing rules that apply to quantitative data are not necessarily appropriate for qualitative data for several reasons. Analysis of qualitative data is inherently interpretive and hinges on a relationship between those conducting the research and their participants, thus making it problematic to share the data widely or conduct secondary analyses in the same manner as with quantitative data. This should be addressed early in the REA planning process. We discuss the issues of data sharing more in detail in the last section on challenges and potential solutions.

Additionally, decisions about publication of REA findings should be grounded in principles of sound and ethical scientific writing. There are good reasons for publishing the results of REAs more widely than is currently customary. Because REAs draw on the actual words of persons affected by the problem, they often shed light on processes, motivations, and values that are not well understood or that have yet to be documented in a systematic way. In this way, they can complement more traditional data collection efforts such as epidemiological and behavioral studies or disease surveillance.

At the same time, the limitations of REAs should be acknowledged in the report and during dissemination when appropriate. Authors should take care that findings are linked to the data, and that recommendations stem from findings. They should take caution not to overstate the results or to jump to conclusions that are not borne out in the analysis.

Writing the REA report—presenting key findings

In most cases, the REA team will be responsible for producing a written report of findings based on the analysis of ethnographic interviews and observational data, plus any data collected through mapping or brief street intercept surveys. Reports can vary in length based on the project but in general a report should be both thorough and concise.

Depending upon how teams are organized and how community members have been engaged in the process, there should be continuity between the field, analysis, and writing teams. There are many ways to do this. Although in most cases it is not possible to engage the entire field team in "hands on" analysis and writing the report, it is good practice to have some community members who were engaged in field work also involved in analysis and report writing. One way to do this is to develop summary tables of key findings or memos that can be shared with community and field team members to obtain their feedback when producing the final report. This should be done at intervals during the analysis and writing process, as well as during the development of recommendations. This helps to ensure that community members' views and perspectives help to inform the final products and that confusion or inaccuracies are cleared up prior to finalizing the report. It does not, however, mean that the interpretation of findings will be changed. We cover this in detail later in this chapter.

At a minimum, the report should include the following information:

1 Background and purpose of the REA.
2 A description of the REA methods, including basic approach, data collection methods used, and the composition of the REA team, along with mention of necessary approvals and process.
3 Timeline—when and where the data were collected and over what period of time.
4 A description of the main findings, including relevant participant characteristics (e.g., social demographics and pertinent roles).
5 Discussion of the main findings (themes, etc.) and conclusions.
6 Any limitations.
7 Recommendations stemming from findings.

Recommendations that stem from the findings should be focused, concise, and actionable. In addition, any relevant appendices, references, and acknowledgments should be included. An executive summary of one to three pages may also be required.

The report should begin with a "Background" section that provides the background and purpose of the REA. This is a summary of the problem, along with a succinct review of the most current available and relevant data and literature on the topic. After reading this section, a reader should have a clear understanding of why the REA was conducted and its main objectives.

Although an exhaustive literature review may not be necessary for a focused report, this section should provide enough context for the reader to know what gaps the REA was intended to fill. It should provide a brief history of the problem or phenomena in question and use established sources and previous studies to contextualize the problem and support the rationale for the REA. A clear statement of purpose will focus the reader's attention on what the REA was meant to accomplish and why it was called for. In some assessments, there may also be a need to elucidate the theoretical or conceptual framework through which the assessment was guided.

Next, a "Methods" section should describe the overall process of data collection: which methods were used and who used them. It should let the reader know where and when the REA took place and how long it took to collect the data. Many readers will be unfamiliar with REA; therefore, this section should briefly describe the overall methodological approach of REA and provide some general sense of how REAs have been used in the past. This helps orient the reader to what comes next.

The "Methods" section should inform the reader as to the specifics of the methods being used and the general conduct and process of interviewing. Were only in-depth interviews conducted, or did the team also conduct focus groups or both? Were street intercept surveys carried out, and if so, where did these take place? Where were the interviews conducted? Were they conducted in homes, in an office, or in some other place? What, in general, were the topics covered in interviews? Where were observations collected and for what purpose? Describe also any mapping that was carried out and how it was used in the project. If tokens of appreciation were given to participants, these also need to be mentioned. Describe how informed consent was obtained. Further, details of direct or participant observation need to be clarified. Where, when (dates and times), and how were observation activities conducted?

The "Methods" section should also describe the type of sampling used, how participants were recruited, and any inclusion and exclusion criteria used. Some brief discussion of the team—who they are in terms of expertise and the agencies or institutions they represent—as well as some discussion of how team interviewing and observation were conducted is also necessary. The methods section should also explain the analysis process: Were interviews and observations recorded and transcribed? Was QDA software used? How many people worked on the analysis and the writing of the report? How was coding handled and managed?

The goal of the "Methods" section is to help the reader get the "big picture" of the REA—who was involved, what they did, and how various tasks were accomplished. If there were consultations or stakeholder meetings leading up to the REA, this is the place to lay those out and describe them if they are relevant. The reader deserves to know which institutions or agencies were involved in the planning process, and what the source of funding was, because all of these relationships have some bearing on how the REA was developed and how the findings may be used. If steps were taken to inform and engage community members more broadly, describe these as well. Note any institutional approvals that were required and granted.

There is no one correct way to write up the findings from the REA; the organization of the findings will be based on the results of the analysis. However, the "Findings" section should include a description of the participants, letting the reader know how many participants there were and any relevant characteristics such as demographic data or professional role. The main body of the report will be a description of what was learned; the main themes and findings that emerged from the REA data analysis. Although there are many different ways to organize and present the key themes and findings that resulted from the qualitative analysis, be sure that these connect to the main research question or focus of the REA. Be descriptive and explanatory when laying out themes and supporting material. Support important interpretations with descriptive narrative and diverse quotes that provide evidence for your interpretations. Write a descriptive narrative around interpretations and research question(s). There may be material from interviews that, although interesting, is not germane to the research questions. Avoid bogging down the report with information that may not be relevant. Stick to presenting evidence for the interpretation and try to be as specific as possible. If the focus of the REA is to explore drug use among a given population, be sure to describe which drugs were used, where and how they were used, and in what contexts. One of the most frequent criticisms of REAs is that they are too diluted or vague (e.g., "We already knew that."). REAs should add depth to what is known in the form of clear description or deep insight.

Direct quotes from ethnographic interviews or observations should be used to describe or illustrate important points; however, take care not to inadvertently identify speakers who have been promised confidentiality by what they say or how they describe themselves or their professional role. Be sure that quotes actually illustrate the point being made in the report. Too often we see novice researchers make a substantive point, and then follow this with a quote that does not illustrate the point at all. Think about whether the quote taken out of context will convey the desired information to a reader. Will it be illustrative? Quotes should also be used sparingly; the interpretation and analysis should make up the bulk of the report, with quotes used to demonstrate important points. Quotes should also reflect a variety of participants from across the study sample. Often in REAs, as in other qualitative studies, there are a few interviews or observations that are particularly rich and compelling. Quotes from these interviews and observations can be quite powerful and persuasive when included in a report. Beware, however, of including too many quotes from one participant. Ensure that quotes are balanced throughout the report and that the perspectives of multiple participants are represented.

REAs often yield unexpected, but significant, findings. This occurs when important information is inadvertently discovered during the course of the REA.

For example, in one REA we learned that sex workers who carried more than one condom risked being arrested. Local police used the carrying of more than one condom as evidence of sex workers' participation in illegal activity. Although this was not the focus of the REA, this unexpected finding was important because it hindered local HIV/STD prevention efforts. Including this in the REA report enabled the local HIV/STD program to work with their police department to discourage this practice.

The team writing the report should assume that it will be shared widely with program managers, policy makers, and stakeholders. Language should be clear and non-judgmental, and devoid of disciplinary jargon. Not everyone will be happy with the findings in the report; often findings highlight problems or shortcomings in service delivery or program management that may make some readers react defensively. When writing the report, be honest about what was learned from the participants, whether it seems negative or not. At the same time, maintain a constructive tone, and avoid casting blame on particular persons or programs. It is essential that even negative feedback be used as an opportunity to improve the overall situation. Be specific about what was learned and what participants said about the problem. When possible, provide clear examples.

Throughout the report, present data and information in a visually appealing manner that the intended audience can readily understand. Use tables, maps, and charts to summarize data and concept models or mind maps to help convey complex ideas or relationships. Data visualizations in the form of tables, graphics, or concept models can help convey the main ideas and findings of the REA. For our REA on sex work in the rural South, we developed a conceptual model that helped illustrate the mobility patterns and "flows" of female sex workers and migrant men. This concept model developed through the process of analysis, team discussions about emerging patterns in the data, and the writing of the report. The model helped us encapsulate what we learned in the field and through our interviews.

Illustrations and photographs taken as part of field observations can also help ground the report findings in the "real" world. Exercise caution, however, when using photographs of persons, locations, or activities that could incriminate or put individuals or populations at risk. Although we photographed locations where sex work reportedly took place, the precise locations were not included in the report due to concerns that this information would increase risk of arrest or harassment.

In a final section, "Conclusions," state the main conclusions in relation to research question(s) and REA purpose, including how findings relate to any conceptual or theoretical arguments. Describe the implications of your findings for the program or the field, and pose new questions if data suggest unforeseen results. Add main discussion points and questions for future research. Finish with a "Limitations" section that shows how the boundaries of the sample, research site, timing, methodology, and analysis limited or enhanced results. A common criticism of qualitative research and REAs is that results are not "generalizable." This statement is not entirely accurate. Although it is true that REAs do not result in findings based on statistical probabilities, they often produce valuable insights and lessons that are useful and applicable to other programs and jurisdictions.

Provide a reference list that includes all citations used. Be accurate and precise so that readers can locate your sources. If there are additional forms, data, or illustrations that were pertinent to the analysis, include them in an organized appendix.

Writing recommendations

REAs can generate a long list of recommendations, and it can be quite challenging to decide how to frame and prioritize them. Recommendations can apply to different levels or multiple scales of intervention—for example, some recommendations will apply directly to the program or agency level, while others may be more relevant to the state or even federal level. In addition, while some recommendations will emerge during the process of data analysis and writing, other recommendations may directly stem from participants, as they share their views on what would improve the program or what should happen related to a given situation.

Conclusions and recommendations should be based directly on the findings of the REA. Some readers may read the recommendations first, before turning to the report; therefore, it is important to write these carefully, as they represent a key aspect of the REA report (see Box 6.1). Although it may be tempting to make broad, sweeping recommendations, these may be beyond the scope or ability of the program to implement. Recommendations will not be useful unless they can be linked to findings presented in the report. They should be concise, focused, and achievable; that is, some action can be undertaken to implement the recommendation. Thinking about the feasibility and acceptability of recommendations—whether there are substantial barriers or underlying strengths, and whether the recommendations would be agreeable

---

Box 6.1

What makes a good recommendation?

- Describes a suggested course of action to be taken to remediate a specific problem
- Conveys achievable action statements
- Uses clear language
- Details done logically, in order of importance or critical need
- Builds directly on findings in the report
- Ideally, incorporates input from project stakeholders and community members

to the various stakeholders—will help keep them grounded and practical. Some recommendations may be important but will be unachievable because of a lack of resources or time. Other recommendations, although valid, may be beyond the power of a program or agency to implement. Consider the various audience(s) for the recommendations and craft them accordingly.

Recommendations that are too "high-level" or too vague or general are not helpful because they deter people from feeling like they can take action. Avoid statements like, "Improve communication," "Provide more education about X," or "Develop structural interventions to reduce disparities." Statements such as these are too broad to be of much use to a program, unless there are more concrete details associated with them. Be as specific as possible and provide examples and potential actions that can be taken. During a REA of syphilis among MSM, our analysis showed that MSM's perceptions of syphilis affected their clinical and social experience of syphilis and hindered disclosure and partner notification, contributing to uncertainty and confusion about disease acquisition, transmission risk, and risk-reduction strategies. Rather than just recommending that the program, "Improve communication about syphilis," we compiled a list of topics gleaned from in-depth interviews and conversations with MSM and with program staff who interacted with clients. We were able to include these in a table in the report, which enabled the program to respond in a more focused and specific way than had they just been given a general statement about improving messaging around syphilis.

There are various ways to present recommendations based on the project and report. It is usually helpful to identify a few major findings in the report to which specific recommendations can be linked (see examples in Chapter 7). At other times, it may be useful to present recommendations in the form of a table that lists long and short-term recommendations, and that indicates which level of organization (e.g., local, state, federal) should logically be responsible for implementing the recommendation. When writing up recommendations, it can be useful to think through who the recommendation is meant to benefit and to lay out a few steps that can be taken by the program, along with some evaluation measures (see Table 6.1). It is often a good idea to begin with short-term recommendations—those that

Table 6.1 Recommendation matrix

Finding	Recommendation	Target Population	Action Plan	Evaluation Measures
Prenatal care providers do not have access to a ready supply of bicillin to treat pregnant women with syphilis	Ensure that priority providers have access to bicillin	Pregnant women in a syphilis high morbidity area	Conduct provider visitation. Develop plan for delivering bicillin to key providers	# provider visits made # of women treated with bicillin supplied by the STD program

can be easily implemented—and end with more complex or long-term recommendations, giving the list a logical flow and making it easier for program
administrators and decision makers to see which recommendations they can
prioritize or take immediate action on. More frequent experiences of success in implementing short-term recommendations result in greater motivation for individuals and institutions to search for better strategies and to plan
ahead for acting on long-term recommendations. Listing recommendations
this way allows readers to make connections between short-term and long-
term recommendations, underscoring how achieving short-term goals along
the way can improve chances of reaching longer-term solutions.

What is the dissemination plan for findings?

REAs are meant to be timely and practical. REAs in which the analysis
and report writing drag on for months, or even years, run the risk of being
overtaken by subsequent events and becoming irrelevant. Many things can
happen during the labor-intensive months of analysis and writing. For example, funding runs out, new management arrives, the program takes a different
direction, or the epidemic continues unabated. For this reason, we recommend that a final written report be the first product to be compiled and delivered promptly to key stakeholders and decision makers. This ensures that
they learn about key findings and recommendations of the REA in a timely
manner. Waiting to publish the findings in a peer-reviewed manuscript can
take months or sometimes years of valuable time.

Funders, managers, and stakeholders are usually eager to learn about findings as soon as fieldwork has ended. We recommend engaging them in the
process and keeping them informed as to progress along the way. We often
provided a brief exit summary or conference call with the program at the end
of fieldwork. This allowed the REA team to share some preliminary impressions, with the caveat that analysis had yet to take place and things could
change. Discussions such as these can be a catalyst for programs to begin
planning for needed changes and adjustments.

In most projects, we provided a draft report to a small group of stakeholders so that findings and draft recommendations could be discussed before
the report was finalized and disseminated for wider circulation. As mentioned earlier, this process helped us learn whether the findings had internal
validity—in other words, did they "ring true" with program staff and community members? It also allowed for discussion and input of draft recommendations. Because REAs take place in a limited time frame, there can be gaps
in what the REA team understands about what is said or observed. These
conversations with program staff often resulted in needed clarifications and
an improved final report.

Because ethnographic and qualitative research is largely based on interpretive and contextual data, findings need to be consistent and credible if they
are to be useful to programs or communities. Therefore, the REA needs

to seriously consider issues of validity and credibility. We refer to internal validity as accuracy and trustworthiness of the findings (Altheide and Johnson 1994; Miller 1986). In qualitative work, this largely depends on the richness and quality of data collected (rather than quantity), and whether participants feel that the findings of the REA accurately reflect the phenomena being studied. Multiple forms of triangulation—cross-checking information from multiple perspectives—also can help verify the strength of REA findings.

Once the final report has been delivered to funders, the main work of the REA may be done. However, the REA team can play an important role in encouraging the program to disseminate the findings more broadly. In our work with state health departments, we strongly encouraged them to present the REA findings to local stakeholders in the form of a town-hall meetings, which allowed others from the community to come together and discuss the implications of the findings. These discussions sometimes resulted in new collaborations and additional actions taken by the program and its partners.

Delivery of the final report is often followed up by broader dissemination in the form of presentations at scientific conferences and publication of peer-reviewed manuscripts in academic or applied research journals.

What is the follow-up plan?

Ideally, the REA has contributed to "an understanding of the current situation—strengths, threats, and capacity to respond—used to inform the direction of future planning" (Kroeger, Torrone, and Nelson 2016). As part of the final report, it is advisable to include a proposed follow-up plan to provide additional guidance and support to the program and its stakeholders. For example, the program may have additional technical assistance needs related to the recommendations. The REA team may be able to link them to appropriate experts, or to help them identify training or other resources. Because reports often end up in a desk drawer and busy programs may ignore recommendations, it can be useful to make a plan to check in with the program periodically through calls or visits. This can be frustrating at times, but it can also help keep momentum going. In most cases, the work of the REA team is mainly to collect data and compile the results in a way that informs the program and helps them move in a desired direction. Once the work is done, the REA team's work is over. However, continued engagement and collaboration with the program may be appropriate and valued, and a follow-up plan, however brief, sets the stage for this discussion.

In one case, this meant linking local health department staff to physicians at a teaching hospital interested in providing research assistance. The REA team made introductions and checked in with the program periodically to learn how things were progressing. In another REA, a team member helped plan a town-hall meeting and acted as a facilitator. In a large, multi-site REA, members of the team worked with government and non-government organizations to plan for regional meetings in which results of the REA were presented. They also assisted stakeholders with developing proposals to secure funding for community-based interventions. Later, when funding was secured, members of the REA team provided training and helped develop evaluation plans.

Challenges and potential solutions

Data sharing

Data are being increasingly collected and drawn from a number of new sources as data-intensive research and "big data" analytics (e.g., vital statistics, electronic health records, internet searches) gain ground (Fecher, Friesike, and Hebing 2015). As a result, data are perceived as valuable and shareable commodities that have tremendous potential to advance research and innovation, maximizing public investments in research and education (Mannheimer et al. 2019). Policies instituted by federal funding agencies, private funders, academic institutions, and peer-reviewed journals increasingly encourage data sharing. In education, health-related, and social science scholarship, most data sharing has been within the context of quantitative survey data, which are often used to conduct secondary analysis. Increasingly, however, qualitative researchers are also being encouraged to share their data for reuse and secondary analysis (Heaton 2008).

Sharing qualitative data brings about unique and complex challenges (McGrath and Nilsonne 2018; Tsai et al. 2016). For instance, there is concern that data will be compromised if they are removed from their original context and then analyzed by others who were not involved in designing and conducting the original research project (Van den Berg 2008). As we discussed earlier, qualitative research, particularly ethnographic work, is rooted in complex relations between researchers and participants, where data are co-constituted and created through such interactions. Sharing data, therefore, may not be a decision that is for researchers to make alone, and should involve participants. Further, other scholars have pointed to additional ethical challenges regarding issues related to informed consent, confidentiality, and anonymity when sharing qualitative data for secondary use (Bishop 2009; Broom, Cheshire, and Emmison 2009).

Some potential solutions to these challenges include planning for and obtaining informed consent from participants for future uses beyond the original research team (Mannheimer et al. 2019). Academic data repositories and libraries may be able to assist in helping the REA team create ethically-oriented data management and sharing plans (Cliggett 2013). They may also be able to provide various levels of restricted access to data that cannot be completely anonymized. Data repositories and academic libraries are not perfect solutions for many concerns related to data sharing expressed by qualitative researchers, especially in the contexts in which REA may take place, but they can be helpful in working through complex issues with individual researchers and REA teams who may be required to consider data sharing.

Data sharing issues should be considered early in the process, during the planning phase in consultation with key stakeholders, funders, and others to whom the REA team is accountable. Speaking to those who work and manage data repositories and librarians is advisable. The REA team must also be prepared to factor in any costs associated with data storage and sharing in their budget planning.

Disagreement about findings

REAs are based on a set of relations—among team members, between the REA team and participants, and between the REA team and its funders, sponsors, or stakeholders; as such, there is always a chance for disagreements. During the dissemination and reporting out phase, there may be disagreements or negative reactions to findings that result from the REA. For instance, a program manager may take issue with a particular finding that points to clients not utilizing clinical services due to structural barriers such as experiences of provider discrimination or difficulty booking a timely appointment. They may simply express disagreement or attempt to convince you that their view of the facts in the only correct view, that their position is the "right" one.

Although it is rare, some audience members such as funders may ask that certain results and findings be removed or changed in the report so they do not reflect badly on a particular program, institution, or individual in charge. These types of exchanges can be detrimental because they can sidetrack everyone from seeking solutions that will be in the best interest of those most impacted by the issue at hand. Often, these arguments amount to a breakdown in communication, and there are some effective ways to deal productively with such disagreements. There should be a distinction made between member checking, where details might be changed for accuracy, and someone who is not a participant, like a manager, asking for a change in the report's results and findings. Even though funders, sponsors, and stakeholders should not determine research findings, insights, or recommendations of the assessment, ultimately, the REA is accountable to them, and this is sometimes where the pressure to modify findings comes from.

When an audience member or members express their disagreement, it is best to gain an understanding of their point of view and be willing to listen to their concerns. This can be done by scheduling individual or group meetings to build empathy and gain an understanding of their position, interests, and priorities. Empathy is a respectful and relatively neutral stance and it does not imply support for the person's position.

Reiterate the purpose of the REA and explain the REA team's strong commitment to providing helpful and effective information that is actionable. It may be helpful to go over the REA report together and discuss more thoroughly specific findings and recommendations. Emphasize that the REA findings are meant to provide a starting point for discussion and potential changes to improve the overall program. As stated earlier, writing that is clear and non-judgmental in tone may make readers less defensive. Offering context for why some negative observations are in the report—the reasons behind things (e.g., nurses are unhappy because the program has been short-staffed for months)—may help individuals focus on the problem rather than feel blamed.

Often, you can help your colleagues understand that although there may be different points of view, there are ways to effectively address issues. If there is still conflict, welcome comments, suggestions, and engagement to enhance the quality of REA findings. For instance, ask if they have additional recommendations that could be incorporated into the report. Work with them to come to a mutually acceptable solution. Do not, at any point, give in to pressure to change or omit substantive findings to fit someone else's preference. It is important to maintain the independence of the REA even if funders disagree with findings and conclusions.

In some cases, people may fear being blamed, disciplined, or fired because of what they perceive to be findings that reflect negatively on them or their program. However, in the majority of cases, REAs have served to document problems in a way that is ultimately helpful to programs. Rather than feeling blamed or criticized, managers and administrators have often used the REA report as a tool to help them "report up" to managers and policy makers—as a way of providing evidence that problems exist. This documentation has been used to help them advocate for more resources or to persuade decision makers to make necessary changes.

Publishing obstacles

Because REAs are accountable to multiple constituents, including funders, communities, and institutions, there may be obstacles that arise related to wide dissemination of findings. During the planning phase, the REA team needs to make sure that all ethical requirements are met (e.g., IRB, informed consent, etc.). The team should also ensure that dissemination plans are discussed and agreed upon before the REA begins. This includes who can publish or present information that results from the REA. Pay close attention to whether any products related to the REA need to have authorization or oversight before they can be disseminated. For instance, government agencies, funders, or other institutions may require a pre-review process to get approval before publishing or presenting findings. This can, at times, slow down the dissemination process, or even prevent work from being published.

Additionally, REAs are examples of practical applied work, and team members who wish to publish or present findings may find it challenging to locate suitable publishing or presentation venues. Conferences and peer-reviewed publishing outlets, especially those with an applied, programmatic, or policy focus, often welcome REA work. There may be obstacles, however, in publishing and presenting at more academically focused publishing and conference venues, because of the rapid, applied nature of REAs. This can be both frustrating and discouraging. We encourage REA practitioners and teams, as well as programs that have benefited from REAs to present, publish, and disseminate their work widely; currently, the results of few REAs are published. This needs to change. Practitioners of REA need outlets for this work to expand awareness of and knowledge about REA, strengthen methodological rigor, and encourage others to adopt its use. Finding reputable journals and conferences that value innovative methodological, engaged research practices and analysis focused on providing solutions to practical problems will go a long way towards this effort.

Box 6.2

Summary

- The REA team is responsible for producing a written report of findings that describes the project and its findings, along with any recommendations that stem from the findings.
- The final report should be structured into key sections and use clear, non-judgmental language.
- Recommendations should be based directly on the findings of the REA, and include practical, actionable items.
- The REA team can play an important role in encouraging the program to disseminate the findings more broadly.
- The final report should ideally include a proposed follow-up plan to provide additional guidance and support to the program and its stakeholders.

References

Altheide, David L., and John M. Johnson. 1994. Criteria for assessing interpretive validity in qualitative research. In *Handbook of Qualitative Research*, edited by Norman K. Denzin and Yvonna S. Lincoln, 485–499. Thousand Oaks, CA: Sage.

Bishop, Libby. 2009. Ethical sharing and reuse of qualitative data. *Australian Journal of Social Issues* 44(3): 255–272.

Broom, Alex, Lynda Cheshire, and Michael Emmison. 2009. Qualitative researchers' understandings of their practice and the implications for data archiving and sharing. *Sociology* 43(6): 1163–1180.

Cliggett, Lisa. 2013. Qualitative data archiving in the digital age: Strategies for data preservation and sharing. *The Qualitative Report* 18(24): 1–11.

Fecher, Benedikt, Sascha Friesike, and Marcel Hebing. 2015. What drives academic data sharing? *PloS ONE* 10(2): e0118053.

Heaton, Janet. 2008. Secondary analysis of qualitative data: An overview. *Historical Social Research* 33(3): 33–45.

Kroeger, Karen, Elizabeth Torrone, and Robert Nelson. 2016. Assessment: A core function for implementing effective interventions in sexually transmitted disease programs. *Sexually Transmitted Diseases* 43(2Suppl1): S3–7.

Mannheimer, Sara, Amy Pienta, Dessislava Kirilova, Colin Elman, and Amber Wutich. 2019. Qualitative data sharing: Data repositories and academic libraries as key partners in addressing challenges. *American Behavioral Scientist* 63(5): 643–664.

McGrath, Cormac and Gustav Nilsonne. 2018. Data sharing in qualitative research: opportunities and concerns. *MedEdPublish* 7(4): 34.

Miller, Marc L. 1986. *Reliability and Validity in Qualitative Research*. Thousand Oaks, CA: Sage.

Tsai, Alexander C., Brandon A. Kohrt, Lynn T. Matthews, Theresa S. Betancourt, Jooyoung K. Lee, Andrew V. Papachristos, Sheri D. Weiser, and Shari L. Dworkin. 2016. Promises and pitfalls of data sharing in qualitative research. *Social Science & Medicine* 169: 191–198.

Van den Berg, Harry. 2008. Reanalyzing qualitative interviews from different angles: The risk of decontextualization and other problems of sharing qualitative data. *Historical Social Research* 33(3): 179–192.

7 Case studies

Key learning outcomes

1 Recognize range, size, and scope of REAs
2 Understand how REAs have been used to investigate problems
3 Be familiar with how recommendations link to findings
4 Identify potential follow-up activities and outcomes from REAs

In this chapter, we provide three case studies based on REAs. Two examples are drawn from REAs we conducted as part of our work as government anthropologists working on public health issues in the United States; the third example is based on a large, multi-site international REA that was led by the Medical Research Council in South Africa with the Centers for Disease Control and Prevention (CDC) providing technical support and funding.

Our purpose in presenting these case studies is to ground material in the book in "real-world" examples of how REAs have been used to help communities and programs explore and then respond to problems. Our knowledge of these REAs comes from first-hand experience and substantive participation in these projects. This means that one or both of us took part in some or all of the following: planning and protocol development; training of field and analysis teams; leading field teams and conducting fieldwork, including conducting interviews, observations, and debriefings; analyzing data; writing reports and manuscripts; developing recommendations; and conveying findings and recommendations to stakeholders and community members. In some cases, we were involved in follow-up activities such as stakeholder meetings to plan interventions, follow-up REAs to assess changes, town halls to share information with wider communities, and other activities.

In what follows, we present an overview or summary of each project with highlighted findings and recommendations, along with notes about activities that took place after the REA. There are also published manuscripts that describe aspects of these projects in more detail. These papers are referenced at the end of each case study.

Case study 1: HIV/STD, sex work, and migrant men in North Carolina

In 2010, we conducted a REA in North Carolina (NC), USA, to better understand the context of interactions between Latino migrant men and female sex workers. The Centers for Disease Control and Prevention, Division of STD Prevention (CDC/DSTDP) received reports from several southern states—including North Carolina, Florida, and Georgia—indicating that female sex workers were moving or being transported throughout the US Southeast. These reports corresponded with studies that indicated that Latino migrant men, a population that is also highly mobile, were engaging in sex with female sex workers while in the United States (Apostolopoulos et al. 2006; Painter 2008). Although some state and local health departments were monitoring HIV/STD prevalence among street-based sex workers, there was little known about how to address the sexual health needs of these highly mobile, and difficult to reach, women. The exploratory REA was a collaboration between the NC Division of Public Health HIV/STD Prevention and Care Branch and the Division of STD Prevention at the CDC. The purpose of the REA was to obtain information about the organization and typology of sex work in select areas of the state, the geographic mobility patterns among female sex workers, and the potential for increased HIV/STD transmission among sex workers and migrant men. Findings were meant to inform the state's HIV/STD prevention efforts.

Design, methods, planning, and implementation

Initial planning discussions with key state-level public health staff in North Carolina took place in January 2010. Program staff members participated in protocol development and provided assistance with identifying local community-based organizations and key informants with knowledge and experience in delivery of health and social services to female sex workers and Latino migrant laborers. These initial discussions were followed by calls with other experts in North Carolina who worked closely with Latino migrant and non-migrant populations. These informational phone interviews generated a list of key informants and provided additional understanding of the local context. The calls also generated interest in and support for the REA. Later, during fieldwork, outreach workers from local community organizations helped facilitate access to migrant housing and brothel locations where the team conducted observations.

The REA team also conducted web-based searches for community-based organizations and agencies serving Latino populations and for local experts from academic institutions. We used Google Earth to identify locations of agencies that worked closely with Latino populations. This type of mapping allowed us to get a sense of the relative locations of the agencies to each other, which helped inform the logistics of the REA. During planning, we scheduled appointments for interviews to take place during the REA, but also left open time in the schedule to interview individuals referred to us during the course of fieldwork and to conduct observations at relevant sites. We also finalized the protocol, logistics, and obtained necessary federal- and state-level human subjects approvals.

We made a decision to focus the assessment on a four-county area surrounding Raleigh due to the presence of social service agencies and substantial numbers of Latino migrant men in the area. For several reasons, we did not attempt to systematically recruit sex workers or their clients for this assessment. Given that this was an exploratory REA focused on informing public health programming, our goal was first to learn as much as we could from health and social service providers who serve these populations. Although providers cannot speak for their clients, they are often valuable, untapped sources of information because they have deep knowledge of the context of their clients' lives, and they often have to make decisions about delivering care in uncertain and difficult policy environments. Finally, given that these populations are hidden and hard to reach, we felt it was necessary to first establish contact with the provider community as they would likely be implementing any future interventions.

The REA took place over one week, from May 17–21, 2010. The REA team consisted of four public health professionals—a public health disease prevention fellow, an epidemiologist with medical training, and two social scientists (the co-authors). Two members of the team had extensive field and public health experience with female sex workers in domestic and international settings. One member spoke Spanish.

Upon arrival in Raleigh we met with Division of Public Health HIV/STD program managers and gave a brief presentation on the project and the schedule for the week. Over the five days, we conducted 28 key informant interviews with persons who had knowledge of or contact with migrant laborers and female sex workers in the four-county area (see Table 7.1). We carried out ten interviews with persons from community-based organizations (CBOs), nine with persons from state and county HIV/STD programs, five with persons from state and local rural health programs, and four with persons who worked in legal services and law enforcement. In addition, we conducted field observations in truck stops, trailer parks, migrant worker camps, and apartment complexes where sex work was reported to take place.

Table 7.1 North Carolina interviews

Type of Organization	Number
CBO	10
State/county HIV/STD	9
State/local rural health	5
Legal/law enforcement	4
Total	28

REA team members worked mainly in pairs; one person served as interviewer while the other took handwritten notes to capture what was being said. Interviews were not recorded; notes were taken verbatim as much as possible and expanded by the interviewer and note taker soon after the interview. Field notes were recorded by hand after each field observation. Before conducting each interview, we informed participants of the purpose of the assessment and obtained verbal consent; all participation was voluntary, and no incentives were given.

We designed interview questions to be open-ended and exploratory, and to elicit participants' views on a range of topics, including perceptions of the typology of sex work, women involved in sex work and their Latino male clients, sexual health-seeking behaviors, and barriers and facilitators to use of HIV/STD prevention services.

Each day, interview pairs conducted three or four interviews; observations took place between interviews and sometimes in the evenings. The entire team met at the end of each day to debrief together, discuss what had been learned that day, and to plan for the next day. Each partner took turns interviewing and taking notes. Interviews were assigned based on topical content and expertise, but also on expediency—geographic location and logistics sometimes dictated interview assignments. Upon return from the field, the team held a conference call with the program to share preliminary impressions and findings, with the caveat that these might change based on the full data analysis.

In the weeks after the REA, the team conducted analysis of qualitative interview data and field notes from observations and debriefing sessions using QSR NVivo 8, a software program to manage qualitative data. Two members of the team wrote the draft report and all four members of the team reviewed and revised sections of the report. All members of the team helped develop recommendations based on the REA; a final draft was sent to the state for review and discussion, and the report was finalized in late 2010.

Summary of main findings

The REA yielded useful information about the organization and typology of sex work in the area and about the degree of mobility among various sectors of the sex-work industry. It also helped program staff and organizations working with Latino migrant men better understand the "geography of sex work"—where, and in what types of venues, sex workers make contact with men and why the potential for risk may be higher among some populations of Latino men than others. These findings have implications for delivery of prevention services.

During interviews, participants described sex workers in terms of race and ethnicity, client base, work location, and mobility factors. Mobility among sex workers and migrant men was a prominent theme, with some sectors of the sex industry characterized by cycles of frequent and wide mobility across a large geographic area ranging from the US Northeast to Florida.

At the other end of the spectrum, non-mobile street-based sex work-ers tended to work in stable locations in urban areas such as Raleigh and smaller suburban towns. These sex workers also had substantial numbers of Latino male clients, although they tended to serve fewer clients than mobile sex workers. Other "locally mobile" women involved in sex work covered smaller geographic areas and worked either independently or with a male partner or "pimp," sometimes traveling to nearby migrant camps and other residential areas with high concentrations of Latino men.

Mobile sex work

Participants said that they were aware of groups of sex workers, mostly Latina women, who were highly mobile, had little autonomy, and were generally hidden and hard to reach. Mobile sex workers usually worked out of brothels, establishments where clients travel to the sex worker. Brothels were located in trailers, houses, and apartment buildings, as well as the back of commercial spaces such as tire repair shops and convenience stores. Brothels were "bare-bones" and frequently moved locations to avoid law enforcement. Clients learned of brothel locations through fliers or business cards passed out in flea markets or other places. Sex workers reportedly charged $20–$30 for services offered in 15-minute increments. Participants reported that brothels housed women working voluntarily as well as trafficked women. Women were rotated to different brothel locations on a weekly or bi-monthly basis; par-ticipants believed that brothel networks were under the control of Mexican criminal organizations and drug cartels, with drugs trafficked along the same pathways as women.

Sex workers were also transported to migrant labor camps at local farms, with sex work taking place in dormitories or specific buildings during the evening hours or on weekends. Because farm workers are usually con-fined to particular housing camps or dormitories and lacked transportation, they were considered a desirable market for sex workers. Outreach workers described small groups of women arriving at camps in unmarked white vans they called "phantom sex vans." These women were often accompanied by men, assumed to be pimps or "padrote." Most women appeared to be in their 20s and Latina, from Mexico and Central or South American coun-tries, with smaller numbers of Caribbean, white, and African American women. Women moved frequently, staying only a week or two in one location, with the frequency of their visits to local labor camps increasing in recent years. Some migrant labor camps have up to 80 or 100 men in them; thus, sex workers were likely servicing high numbers of clients on any given day.

Mobile sex workers also frequented trailer parks and apartment complexes (see Figure 7.1) known to house unaccompanied Latino men employed in sea-sonal or construction work, often going door-to-door. An outreach worker

Figure 7.1 Semi-urban apartment complex, Raleigh, NC.

who approached a group of women he believed were sex workers reported being rebuffed by a man who informed him that the women were "clean" because they had been "certified and screened in New York City."

Non-mobile, street-based sex work

Compared to mobile sex workers, the REA indicated that street-based sex workers were relatively geographically stable and autonomous. Street-based sex workers were based primarily in urban areas of Raleigh and in smaller semi-urban towns on specific streets and locations at predictable times of day or night (see Figure 7.2). Participants described these women as predominantly African American in their 30s and 40s. Street-based sex workers and clients engaged in sex in a variety of venues including the street, in vehicles, behind buildings, and in homes. Many participants stated that they were

Figure 7.2 Street-corner location for sex work, Raleigh, NC.

familiar with locations for street-based sex work in these communities and periodically encountered women involved in sex work. Working in known locations or in particular areas made street-based sex workers more visible and easier to reach by CBOs and health departments.

Service providers told interviewers that street-based sex workers had a diverse client base but sought Latino men as "prime" clients because they were perceived to be less violent than other clients, they were often lonely, and they carried substantial amounts of cash. Street-based sex workers solicited Latino men at gas stations and mechanic shops. They also emphasized that interactions between street-based sex workers and Latino men had increased steadily since 1995, parallel to the construction boom and immigrant population increases in North Carolina.

Street-based sex workers reportedly charged $5–10 for oral sex, $20–30 for vaginal sex, and up to $90 for unprotected anal sex. A participant working with this population estimated that about half of all street-based sex encounters occur without a condom. Participants said that although most street-based sex workers in Raleigh tried to use condoms, a local police practice of interpreting possession of multiple condoms as evidence of soliciting was counterproductive and discouraged some women from carrying them.

Participants emphasized that physical, emotional, and sexual trauma; substance abuse; and mental health issues were common among street-based sex workers. Many experienced housing instability and homelessness, lacked social support, and were isolated from family due to a history of criminal activity and substance abuse. Very few services were available; mental health and substance-abuse treatment programs had few openings, and women with a history of substance abuse were often turned away from domestic violence and homeless shelters.

Other types of venues

Finally, bars and cantinas were also described as venues where sex is exchanged on a more situational, individualized, and sporadic basis. Participants indicated that these venues often employed women, referred to as "ficheras" (ticket, token), to promote alcohol sales in exchange for a share of the profits. A fichera socializes with male patrons and is paid on the basis of how many alcoholic beverages she persuades men to buy. Some ficheras sell sex on a situational basis; for example, at the end of a slow night or if the woman took a liking to a particular man. Ficheras were reportedly a mix of local residents and other, highly mobile women.

Clients of mobile sex workers

Similar to sex workers, many unaccompanied Latino migrant men experience high levels of occupational mobility. Many Latino men are employed as farm workers—the vast majority of these are considered "non-H2A" or working without a temporary guest worker visa (H2A) or documentation of legal residency. These workers have no legal protection, are not formally tied to employers, and are in danger of deportation if apprehended. Their living conditions are unregulated, and they may be at the mercy of "crew leaders" who provide food or housing for a percentage of a worker's wages. Non-H2A workers are vulnerable to exploitation and may move frequently in search of work. Non-H2A workers may be of lower economic status than legally documented workers; they are more fearful of authorities and of using available health services.

In comparison, H2A workers have work visas and legal documentation and are usually tied to one employer during the growing season. Mobility for H2A workers is restricted and they seldom have transportation. They usually reside in dormitories or barracks on or near a farmer's property (see Figure 7.3). Because H2A workers are less mobile and easier to locate than non-H2A workers, they have far more access to health services than do undocumented workers and may even participate in health studies.

Other Latino men migrate in search of non-agricultural work and may work in construction, landscaping, or other fields. Although some men are legal residents; a large majority were thought to lack legal documentation. Regardless, these men also frequent sex workers; construction workers, especially, are sought after because they have more income.

Figure 7.3 H2A migrant housing.

Conclusions

Mobility is a complex construct "encompassing such characteristics as frequency and timing of movement, direction and distance traveled, spatial and geographic range and location, place, or destination" (Sangaramoorthy and Kroeger 2013). Both sex workers and their male Latino clients experience high occupational mobility and may be part of overlapping sexual networks (see Figure 7.4). Contacts, however, between sex workers and clients are not necessarily random; instead, they are structured by the type of venues and work environments that shape their interactions. Sexual networking is a function of numerous social, cultural, economic, and other factors not the least of which are physical space and location, the proximity and availability of sex partners, and venues and locations used to find sex partners.

The 2010 REA documented that contacts between female sex workers and unaccompanied migrant men were common in North Carolina and that potential risk may vary depending on where and when contacts take place. Nearly all participants lamented the dearth of HIV/STD prevention care and treatment services for migrant men and advocated for additional programming and resources to reach them. Some acknowledged that current efforts targeting mainly H2A visa holders amounted to reaching "low hanging fruit" and that far more effort was needed to reach men living in urban areas where interactions take place in multiple types of venues and there

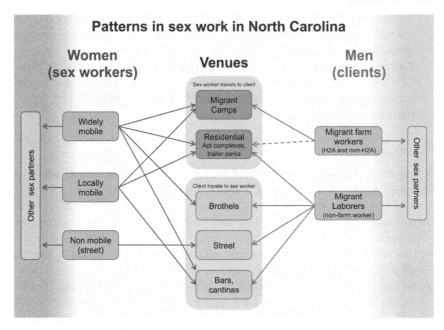

Figure 7.4 Concept model of the geography of sex work in North Carolina.

may be more risk. Participants also emphasized the lack of services targeting female sex workers in all sectors. Program challenges included lack of data and resources, lack of training in how to reach and build rapport with sex workers and their procurers, and a perception that addressing health disparities among Latinos more broadly in North Carolina was not a priority.

Recommendations

- Begin systematic efforts to engage with and build trust between service organizations and mobile sex workers and their procurers or pimps. Conduct additional research and outreach building on HIV/STD intervention models used successfully with sex worker populations in other US jurisdictions and in other countries.
- Increase health education programming among migrant Latino men in camps and in residential areas using culturally appropriate intervention models to increase awareness and reduce the risk of HIV/STD transmission. There are several existing interventions targeting Latino men that can be accessed through CDC and its partners.
- Strengthen outreach programs with street-based sex workers, providing free condoms and HIV/STD testing and linkages to supportive services whenever possible. Engage with local law enforcement to ensure that condoms are not used as evidence of solicitation.

- Ensure that all STD-program clinical staff and disease investigators are trained in the locally established protocol for recognizing and reporting signs of sex trafficking.
- Ensure that timely data on HIV/STD disease burden is shared with partners who work with Latino populations in the state and, to the degree possible, make data available that can help organizations better target their intervention efforts.

Follow-up

In June 2011, the findings of the REA were presented at a Latino Community Forum in North Carolina, along with the findings of a related study carried out by researchers in the state. The forum was supported by the North Carolina Division of Public Health and Wake Forest University. The forum was attended by individuals from government, social service and health agencies, and other community-based advocacy organizations working with Latinos in North Carolina. The forum presented an opportunity for shared learning and a catalyst for collaborative planning among the participants and their organizations.

The findings were also shared through posters and presentations at conferences during 2011 including the National HIV Prevention Conference, the National STD Conference, the East Coast Migrant Stream Conference, and the Society for Applied Anthropology. The co-authors published a peer-reviewed paper based on the assessment in 2013.

References

Apostolopoulos, Yorghos, Sevil Sonmez, Jennie Kronenfeld, Ellis Castillo, Lucia McLendon, and Donna Smith. 2006. STI/HIV risks for Mexican migrant laborers: Exploratory ethnographies. *Journal of Immigrant and Minority Health* 8(3): 291–302.

Painter, Thomas. 2008. Connecting the dots: When the risks of HIV/STD infection appear high but the burden of infection is not known—the case of male Latino migrants in the Southern United States. *AIDS Behavior* 12(2): 213–226.

Sangaramoorthy, Thurka and Karen Kroeger. 2013. Mobility, Latino migrants, and the geography of sex work: Using ethnography in public health assessments. *Human Organization* 72(3): 263–272.

Case study 2: Pathways to congenital syphilis prevention in Caddo Parish, Louisiana

We conducted a REA in 2011 to better understand local factors contributing to increases in syphilis and congenital syphilis (CS) among young African American women in Caddo Parish, Louisiana, USA. The REA was a response to a technical assistance request by the Louisiana Office of Public Health STD/HIV Program. It was designed to: (1) provide better understanding of community and structural-level factors contributing to increases in syphilis and congenital syphilis cases among 15–24-year-old African American women in Caddo Parish, (2) identify factors that affect access to and use of preventive health services among young African American women, and (3) identify strategies for strengthening services to prevent syphilis and congenital syphilis.

Background

Untreated syphilis can result in serious long-term complications for infants. For instance, a woman with untreated syphilis, especially early syphilis, can transmit the infection to her infant during pregnancy which results in perinatal death in at least 40% of cases (CDC 2019). Penicillin is a proven treatment for CS, but prevention measures depend heavily on access to adequate and quality prenatal care that includes syphilis screening and treatment. There are federal and state-level recommendations for syphilis screening and treatment among pregnant women (CDC 2010; CDC 2015), but such guidelines are predicated on the notion that women are receiving timely prenatal care.

Women's use of prenatal care is dependent on a diverse array of psycho-social, behavioral, and structural factors including unplanned or unwanted pregnancy; mental health, substance abuse, or other emotional, family, or personal issues; and lack of access to regular care during pregnancy (Braveman et al. 2000; Feijen-de Jong et al. 2012; Goldenberg et al. 1992; Phillippi 2009). Moreover, missed opportunities within the health system affect women's chances of being screened, tested, and treated for syphilis. While 46 states have laws requiring at least one screening test during pregnancy, only 12 states require screening in the third trimester. Screening in both the first and third trimesters allows providers to monitor the effectiveness of treatment and the patient's response but states requiring additional screening are not necessarily states with the highest morbidity (Hollier et al. 2003).

In the US, CS has largely been concentrated among a small number of states. Most of these are in the South, where case rates are persistently higher than the national case rate. In 2016, CS case rates in the US were disproportionately high among African American women (43.1 cases per 100,000 live births) (CDC 2017; Kroeger et al. 2018). A review of 6383 CS cases reported to the CDC from 1999 to 2013 indicated that most cases (83%) were among infants born to African American or Hispanic mothers. Southern states accounted for more than half of CS cases (52%) in 2013 (Kroeger et al. 2018; Su et al. 2016).

In 2010, Louisiana ranked first among states reporting CS cases, with a case rate of 49.8 cases per 100,000 live births (CDC 2011). The majority of cases were born to African American women (State of Louisiana 2010). As of 2010, Medicaid covered 70% of infant births in the state; with 60% of pregnancies reported as unplanned (State of Louisiana 2011). Analysis of CS cases from 2010 indicated that mothers had limited prenatal care and syphilis testing. Caddo Parish, located in the northwest corner of the state, bordering Arkansas and Texas, had the greatest number of CS cases of any parish in Louisiana (11 of 33 CS cases) in 2010 (State of Louisiana 2010).

Design and methods

Planning for the REA occurred in collaboration with the Louisiana Department of Health. We held phone discussions with state and local HIV/ STD program staff, and with individuals from Caddo Parish community-based organizations to identify key informants and locations relevant to the assessment. The REA team also conducted internet and literature searches to identify other potential informants in academia or service organizations who could provide additional context. Potential participants were contacted by phone, informed about the purpose of the rapid assessment, and asked if they would be willing to participate in interviews during the assessment week. They were also asked to refer other individuals or organizations that provide services to vulnerable women.

The focus of the REA was on eliciting perspectives of individuals who had knowledge of CS and health service challenges experienced by young African American women. We recruited providers of health, social, and other supportive services to African American women in Caddo Parish, along with female clients receiving services. Providers of health and social services interact daily with patients and are often quite knowledgeable about the contexts in which patients live their lives as well as the challenges they encounter in navigating the health system. While providers cannot "speak for" women, they have considerable insight and knowledge to share. Providers also face challenges that affect the way care is delivered to patients.

Participation in interviews was voluntary and no incentives were given. Interview participants provided verbal consent. Interviews were not recorded; instead, handwritten notes were taken during the interview and then expanded by the interview team after the interview. Early in the interview, participants were asked what they thought was most important for us to know regarding increases in syphilis and CS in the Shreveport area. As mentioned earlier, a "grand-tour" question allows the participant to "set the agenda," or shape the direction of the discussion, by disclosing at the beginning of the interview what they, rather than the interviewer, think are the major issues. Following the grand-tour question, participants were asked specific questions regarding: the context of women's lives and how this affects their use of STD and prenatal care services; barriers to prenatal care and syphilis screening and treatment, including challenges providers might be facing; and recommendations for improving delivery of services that prevent syphilis among women. During the REA, the team also conducted field observations in key locations, including the Parish Health Unit during STD clinical hours, a homeless shelter, and a teen mother's high school support group.

Handwritten notes taken during the interviews and observations were later typed into a Microsoft Word template and then imported into NVivo 8, a software program for qualitative data analysis. Two members of the team developed the codebook, coded the data, and developed the draft report. The draft report was reviewed by the remaining members of the team, who provided input and comments. Before finalizing the report, the draft was shared with collaborators in Louisiana and a conference call held to review and discuss recommendations. Ethical review was conducted by the CDC Institutional Review Board.

Main findings

The REA took place in September 2011, and data collection was carried out by a five-person team of public health professionals including both authors. Over a period of five days, 69 people participated in 35 separate interviews; 23 of these were conducted as one-on-one interviews and 12 were carried out as group (coded as 1+ persons) interviews or discussions (see Table 7.2). Of the 69 individual participants, 58 were female and 11 were male; 32 were African American and 37 were white. Interviews or discussions included 14 that took place at with community-based organizational staff; 11 with staff from public and private hospitals or clinics; 6 with Parish Health Unit staff; 2 with correctional setting staff; 1 with a local religious leader; and 1 with a nursing expert. Participants represented a diverse cross-section of persons who provide health and other services to adolescent and young adult African American women in Caddo Parish, including social workers; primary, pre-natal, and STD health-care providers; outreach workers; disease intervention specialists; educators; and community leaders. Two group discussions were held with women, one with teen mothers and one with adult women at a homeless shelter.

Main themes emerging from observation and interviews included: lack of communication, education, and awareness related to sexual health and STDs; social, economic, and health vulnerabilities among young African American women; and barriers and fragmentation in a declining health system.

Table 7.2 Caddo Parish interviews

Participant roles	Number
Clinical—primary or prenatal care	22
Community-based organization manager/staff	14
Social worker/case manager	12
Vulnerable women of childbearing age	10
STD-program staff	4
Correctional center/medical and administrative staff	4
Clinical—STD	3
Total	69

Lack of sexual health communication, education, and awareness

Participants emphasized that there were strong taboos in Caddo Parish against talking openly about sexuality, sexual health, and STDs, including recent syphilis increases. Participants attributed this silence to Caddo Parish's "conservative" and "religious" culture, its location in the Southern Bible Belt, and its rural identity. Participants noted that open discussion of sexual matters was uncommon and that there was considerable stigma associated with STDs. For instance, one participant recounted how board members for a local clinic objected to the clinic's plan to offer STD testing, saying they did not want the clinic to attract "those kinds of people" who might mix with the "regulars." In addition, participants attributed the long history of abstinence-only education mandated in the state to low levels of knowledge and understanding about reproductive and sexual health among adolescents and adults, and to both syphilis and teen pregnancy increases.

Participants also attributed increases in syphilis to broader place-based shifts that increased people's vulnerability to STDs. They perceived the recent growth of the natural gas and casino industries, the city of Shreveport's location in a "wet" county permitting alcohol sales, and the shift from a "rural" to "urban" environment as contextual factors that contributed to a risk environment. Moreover, participants felt that adolescents were particularly vulnerable to these community changes. They expressed concern that state's focus on sexual abstinence rather than comprehensive sexual health education resulted in lack of knowledge among adolescents about reproductive health, pregnancy, and STDs. Without necessary information and skills, adolescents were unlikely to use condoms or contraception, and more likely to engage in unprotected sex.

Participants noted that lack of awareness about syphilis extended to healthcare providers. None of the providers interviewed by the team were aware of receiving alerts or information from regional or state public health officials. Historically, most private providers referred patients needing STD services to the Parish Health Unit. Public sector providers described a "big split" in the medical community in which "private obstetricians don't talk to us and we don't talk to them," again decreasing the likelihood that information about syphilis increases would be shared among providers. Some providers were concerned that the state's shift into a managed-care model meant that private providers would start to see more STD cases and would be ill-equipped to manage them without additional training.

Social, economic, and health vulnerability among young
African American women

Providers characterized their female clients, many of whom were African American, as "working poor" struggling to provide basic necessities for their children while working multiple shifts or jobs. Again, providers stressed that

Figure 7.5 A house in Caddo Parish Public School District.

African American adolescent girls were particularly vulnerable, with complex home lives, often experiencing housing instability, hunger, and food insecurity (see Figure 7.5). Some programs, such as the teen parenting group and the school-based health center the team visited, routinely build provision of food for mothers, infants, and children into their activities. Participants reported that food insecurity had increased significantly over recent years. They noted that intergenerational poverty is common and that many young women suffer from "depression and anxiety due to their stressful home and community life."

They voiced concerns about how such conditions led young women to enter into sexual relationships with men who are considerably older, often exchanging sex for transportation, small amounts of cash, or other material goods. Participants noted that the most recent available data at the time, 2008, indicated that Caddo Parish had a high teen birth rate; 73 per 1000 women compared with the US rate of 40.2 per 1000 women and the Louisiana rate of 54.1 per 1000 women (Annie E. Casey Foundation 2019; Kost, Maddow-Zimet, and Arpaia 2017), with few adolescent girls knowing about pregnancy prevention or care. A participant reported that at least 50–60 students in a local high school were pregnant or already had children. A manager for a teen mothers' support group in the same school said that most girls are months into their pregnancies when they are referred to the group and have yet to see a doctor.

Members of the REA team observed a session of the teen mother support group and spoke with teen mothers. The girls, who ranged in age from 13 to 17, all had children of their own. A 17-year-old high school sophomore was taking care of her own nine-month old child in addition to five younger siblings. Another 17-year-old girl with two children under five years of age said she first became pregnant at 12. Most were not living with the fathers of their children and were raising their children alone. Although some girls were unhappy about their unplanned pregnancies, others expressed their strong desire to become mothers.

Providers described a young woman's relationship with the health-care system as strained and complicated and dependent upon her understanding of the need for preventive and prenatal care, the accessibility of health services, and whether she had a trusting relationship with a provider. Barriers to accessing care were viewed as substantial for some young women, and unless a woman experienced a serious health crisis, she may not seek care. Young women, especially, may not be aware of what constitutes regular preventive care or health risks. Finally, concerns about costs and time associated with transportation, tests, and follow-up work may keep a woman from seeking care.

Barriers and fragmentation in a declining health system

Participants who were health-care providers often spoke in terms of women's agency—the presumption that patients will take an active role in "managing" their health-care needs and are able to "navigate" the health system. However, they also observed that many women were already managing numerous other demands and crises that took precedence. Further, women interviewed by the REA team expressed their frustration with the fragmented and overburdened health system. They described long waits to get appointments and long hours in waiting rooms. Women pointed out that unstable living situations make planning for an appointment six months out nearly impossible. "By the time you see them, you're dead," said a participant who was living in a homeless shelter, indicating that for many women, not being seen in a timely manner can mean not being seen at all. Women also expressed concern about stigma associated with "charity care," "feeling less than and overlooked" as Medicaid patients, and not being given the same respect as patients with private insurance.

In terms of prenatal care, providers felt that there were a variety of reasons why women did not seek services. For instance, if a pregnancy is unplanned or unwanted, a woman may delay seeking care. For women who want care, there were substantial health-system barriers. A lack of referral points, an overburdened public hospital, and difficulty finding providers who take Medicaid made it difficult for some women to access timely prenatal care. At the time of the 2011 assessment, three options for prenatal care existed for women on Medicaid in Caddo Parish: one was the LSU Medical Center, which many women were reluctant to use because of the stigma of "charity care" and the long waits. Some women were able to find one of the few providers in private practice who accepted Medicaid. A third option was the prenatal care clinic operating in the Caddo Parish Health Unit (PHU), which closed for good during the week of the assessment. Although in years past, the Nurse Family Partnership had operated several prenatal care clinics in the Parish, between 2008 and 2011 all of their clinics closed due to a cut in block grant funding, leaving far too few options for women.

Getting care early in a pregnancy is important for CS prevention. The REA found that many poor women have sporadic and discontinuous interactions with the health-care system, and as a consequence, lacked these ongoing relationships. This often meant that women spent considerable time locating a prenatal care provider and were further along in their pregnancies before they had a first prenatal care visit. Providers can choose to take or refuse new Medicaid clients at any given time. For example, a female participant reported that a provider with whom she had a good relationship delivered her first child, but then stopped taking Medicaid, meaning she had to find a different provider for her second pregnancy. This affects the continuity of relationships with providers and the timing of entry into prenatal care.

Many participants expressed concern over the limited amount of time that pregnant women have to establish a relationship with a prenatal care provider. A woman may not immediately realize she is pregnant or may delay seeking care if the pregnancy is unwanted or unplanned. Once she starts looking, she may have trouble finding a provider who will take her. The more delays she experiences, the more her chances of being seen by a provider at all are jeopardized. Most providers will not accept a woman who is past 20 weeks pregnant because they consider the pregnancy high risk. Providers are also reluctant to take women with chronic health conditions. Thus, poor women, many of whom suffer from conditions associated with and exacerbated by poverty (e.g., high blood pressure, diabetes, obesity) have an even harder time finding a prenatal care provider than other women.

Even if a pregnant woman is able to locate a prenatal care provider, in Caddo Parish there were missed opportunities to prevent CS due to problems in the health system. Although screening pregnant women for syphilis was described as routine practice, providers were often unable to treat women due to significant cost and administrative barriers that contributed to delays in timely treatment, resulting in the loss of the patient to follow-up. Low rates of Medicaid reimbursement and lack of coverage under the state's family planning program discouraged most private-practice physicians from providing treatment. Most providers and pharmacies did not keep bicillin on hand due to cost, storage requirements, and low demand.

Some providers wrote prescriptions for bicillin, but few pharmacies carried it. Even if a pharmacy had it, most patients were unwilling or unable to pay the cost. Treatment also required pre-approval from insurance providers, creating another barrier and delay. Finally, some prenatal care providers did not feel adequately trained to handle syphilis cases in pregnant women

Figure 7.6 Caddo Parish Health Unit STD clinic.

due to their complexity. Although prenatal care providers were comfortable diagnosing syphilis, they often referred management of cases to the PHU, increasing the potential loss of a patient to follow-up. At the same time, overburdened PHU staff complained about providers "dumping" patients on public health (see Figure 7.6).

Participants also described gaps in sexual and reproductive health care that affect pre-conception health and reflect the fragmented nature of the health system. Discontinuities and gaps in the Louisiana Children's Health Insurance Program (LaCHIP) caused young women to effectively "age out" of care at the age of 19, after which women needed to meet the income qualification to enroll in Medicaid. Under the state's family planning program, Take Charge, women could get annual reproductive health exams and contraceptives, but not all providers accepted Take Charge, and the program did not cover treatment for some STDs. Pregnant women were eligible to enroll in the state's LaMoms program and receive comprehensive care, but this ended six weeks postpartum.

Conclusions

Interviews with health and social service providers and vulnerable women, along with observations in key field sites, indicated factors at multiple levels that can contribute to CS increases. Although individual-level factors can certainly affect health-care seeking, the assessment showed that there were social, structural, and health-care systems factors that had a negative impact. Taboos against speaking openly about matters related to sexual health and the state's abstinence-only education policy contributed to a lack of basic understanding about pregnancy and STD prevention. Failure to communicate urgent health information about syphilis increases to the provider and broader community contributed to lack of awareness.

In addition to stressors associated with social and economic vulnerability, poor women seeking pre-conception and pregnancy care experienced numerous structural and systems barriers, including discontinuities and gaps in insurance coverage, a dearth of referral points, and difficulty finding providers, including prenatal care providers, who take Medicaid. Impediments such as these may diminish timely opportunities to diagnose and treat pregnant women with syphilis and lead to additional CS cases.

Providers also experienced barriers in treating pregnant women with syphilis, including inadequate training in syphilis case management and insurance and supply-side barriers to obtaining bicillin, the recommended syphilis treatment. Contraction of public health services due to budget shortfalls and the state's plan to shift to a managed-care model indicated that private providers were likely to see more syphilis and CS cases in the future, unless steps were taken to address barriers that hinder care.

Recommendations

Increase awareness and knowledge about syphilis among providers and community members.

- Prioritize key health-care providers for STD-program provider visitation in which information about syphilis increases and treatment guidelines are shared.
- Present information about syphilis at hospital Grand Rounds, and at In-Service clinical staff forums.
- Consider using the state's Health Alert System or another similar channel to disseminate information about syphilis to providers.
- Consider holding town halls or other forums led by local and regional public health leaders and policy makers to share information about syphilis increases, and syphilis prevention and treatment.
- Work with local community and faith-based organizations to increase outreach and education to vulnerable women of child-bearing age and their male partners.

Support and facilitate training opportunities for priority providers.

- Share information with local providers about CDC-funded regional STD Prevention Training Centers to strengthen partnerships and expertise.

- Target prioritized provider specialties in local medical schools and hospitals for STD training, especially family practice, pediatric, adolescent, and emergency medical residents.

Work to remove structural barriers to syphilis treatment and to encourage screening and testing in priority populations.

- Collaborate with the state Medicaid program to remove barriers and gaps in treatment coverage.
- Facilitate delivery of bicillin to priority providers in Caddo Parish.
- Strengthen state statutes to require 3rd trimester syphilis testing in pregnant women.
- Expand screening and treat syphilis in other high priority settings such as correctional facilities and community-based clinics serving vulnerable populations.

Follow-up

The assessment helped to shed light on problems occurring in the health system that affect timely prenatal care and screening and treatment of pregnant women for syphilis. After 2011, the State's Office of Public Health worked with local and state partners to take several steps to improve pathways for CS prevention. These included forming a parish-level Syphilis Prevention Task Force that included individuals from local community health, social service, and faith-based organizations, along with experts from Louisiana State University's Medical Center. The Task Force developed a three-year plan that included outreach and communications activities. Regional and local PHU staff made over 175 provider visits, sharing information and guidelines. Additional channels were used to disseminate information about syphilis increases and screening and treatment guidelines, including the state's Health Alert System. The state also took several steps to strengthen and expand syphilis testing and treatment, including working with the state's five managed-care insurance providers to eliminate pre-approval requirements for treatment; expanding coverage under Take Charge; and helping qualifying facilities obtain necessary certification that facilitated additional community-based syphilis testing. The state also passed legislation mandating syphilis testing for pregnant women in the first and third trimesters. In 2015, the CDC collaborated with Louisiana to conduct a follow-up REA to document progress and changes in Caddo Parish. The REA also resulted in a published manuscript co-authored by CDC and Louisiana partners.

References

Annie E. Casey Foundation. 2019. "Teen birth rate: ages 15-19 in Louisiana." Baltimore, MD: KIDS COUNT Data Center. Accessed on January 8, 2020. https://datacenter. kidscount.org/data/tables/1561-teen-birth-rate-ages-15-19#detailed/2/any/false/ 871,870,573,869,36,868,867,133,38,35/any/3329,7826.

Braveman, Paula, Kristen Marchi, Susan Ergeter, and Michelle Pearl. 2000. Barriers to timely prenatal care among women with insurance: the importance of pre-pregnancy factors. *Obstetrics and Gynecology* 95(6 Pt 1):874–80.

Centers for Disease Control and Prevention (CDC). 2010. Congenital syphilis–United States 2003–2008. *Morbidity and Mortality Weekly Report* 59(14): 413–417.

Centers for Disease Control and Prevention (CDC). 2011. "Sexually transmitted disease surveillance 2010." Atlanta: U.S. Department of Health and Human Services. Accessed on January 8, 2020. https://www.cdc.gov/std/stats/archive/surv2010.pdf

Centers for Disease Control and Prevention (CDC). 2015. Sexually transmitted diseases treatment guidelines. *Morbidity and Mortality Weekly Report* 64(RR-3):1–137.

Centers for Disease Control and Prevention (CDC). 2017. "Sexually transmitted disease surveillance 2016." Atlanta: U.S. Department of Health and Human Services. Accessed on January 8, 2020. http://www.cdc.gov/std/stats12/toc.htm

Centers for Disease Control and Prevention (CDC). 2019. "Congenital syphilis: CDC fact sheet." Atlanta: U.S. Department of Health and Human Services. Accessed January 8, 2020. https://www.cdc.gov/std/syphilis/stdfact-congenital-syphilis.htm

Feijen-de Jong, Esther I., Danielle Jansen, Frank Baarveld, Cees P. van der Schans, François G. Schellevis, and Sijmen A. Reijneveld. 2012. Determinants of late and/or inadequate use of prenatal healthcare in high-income countries: a systematic review. *European Journal of Public Health* 22(6): 904–913.

Hollier, Lisa M., James Hill, Jeanne S. Sheffield, and George D. Wendel Jr. 2003. State laws regarding prenatal syphilis screening in the United States. *American Journal of Obstetrics and Gynecology* 189(4): 1178–1183.

Goldenberg, Robert L., Ellen Tate Patterson, and Margaret Frees. 1992. Maternal demographic, situational and psychosocial factors and their relationship to enrollment in prenatal care: a review of the literature. *Women's Health* 19(2–3):133–151.

Kost, Kathryn, Issac Maddow-Zimet, and Alex Arpaia. 2017. "Pregnancies, births and abortions among adolescents and young women in the United States, 2013: national and state trends by age, race and ethnicity". New York: Guttmacher Institute. Accessed on January 8, 2020. https://www.guttmacher.org/report/us-adolescent-pregnancy-trends-2013

Kroeger, Karen, Thurka Sangaramoorthy, Penny Loosier, Rebecca Schmidt, and DeAnn Gruber. 2018. Pathways to congenital syphilis prevention: A rapid qualitative assessment of barriers, and the public health response in Caddo Parish, Louisiana. *Sexually Transmitted Diseases* 45(7): 442–446.

Phillippi, Julia C. 2009. Women's perceptions of access to prenatal care in the United States: A literature review. *Journal of Midwifery &Women's Health* 54(3): 219–225.

State of Louisiana. 2010. "2010 STD/HIV program report." New Orleans, LA: Louisiana Department of Health and Hospitals, Office of Public Health STD/HIV Program. Accessed on January 8, 2020. http://ldh.la.gov/assets/oph/HIVSTD/hiv-aids/Annual_Reports/2010SHPFINAL042012.pdf

State of Louisiana. 2011. "Louisiana medicaid annual report: state fiscal year 2010–2011." New Orleans, LA: Louisiana Department of Health and Hospitals. Accessed January 1, 2020. http://new.dhh.louisiana.gov/assets/medicaid/AnnualReports/Medicaid_10_11_fnl.pdf

Su, John, Lesley C. Brooks, Darlene W. Davis, Elizabeth A. Torrone, Hillard S. Weinstock, and Mary Kamb. 2016. Congenital syphilis: trends in mortality and morbidity in the United States, 1999 through 2013. *American Journal of Obstetrics and Gynecology* 214(3): 381.e1–381.e9.

Case study 3: Rapid assessment of drug use and sexual HIV risk patterns among vulnerable drug-using populations in Cape Town, Durban, and Pretoria, South Africa

Background

In 2005, a rapid ethnographic assessment, using the International Rapid Assessment and Response Evaluation (I-RARE) model of REA, was undertaken in three South African cities. In 2004, South Africa had the highest prevalence rate of HIV in the world; 29.5% among antenatal clinic attendees (Statistics South Africa 2006), with an estimated 5.5 million of the country's population living with HIV, according to UNAIDS (2006). Numerous studies had already documented increases in injection and non-injection drug use, along with the use of drugs in sex work, yet little attention had been paid to preventing the spread of HIV among these populations. Regional and local initiatives, including the drafting of a National Drug Master Plan, brought attention to the issue and to the dearth of available data on vulnerable drug-using populations. The purpose of the REA was to obtain a better understanding of injecting and non-injecting drug users and of the risk context for HIV transmission and to make recommendations for a public health response.

I-RARE, developed by the Centers for Disease Control and Prevention (CDC), is an adaptation of the RARE model developed by Trotter and colleagues (2001). The project was a collaboration between the CDC and the Medical Research Council of South Africa (MRC), with funding from the US President's Emergency Plan for AIDS Relief (PEPFAR). The Committee for Human Research in the Medical Faculty at the University of Stellenbosch granted ethnical approval.

Design and methods

REAs were carried out in three different cities: Cape Town, Pretoria, and Durban. A planning visit in South Africa enabled the US and South Africa teams to meet and review the available data and discuss priorities for the assessment. It also enabled them to meet with individuals in the Ministry of Health, and with stakeholders in non-government and community-based organizations in all three cities. These meetings not only generated interest in and support for the project but they were also an opportunity for planners to obtain input and advice from local community-based organizations about how best to engage with hidden and hard-to-reach populations in the three cities.

The project employed a full complement of REA methods, including in-depth interviews, focus groups, mapping, observation, and street intercepts. The South Africa project team recruited local community members in each city as field staff. Field team members were of diverse ethnicity and background and included persons who formerly used drugs as well as outreach workers, social workers, lay health advisors, and others. Just prior to the start of data collection, 18 field team members took part in an intensive five-day training in Cape Town. US-based CDC staff provided technical assistance as trainers, with training covering (1) the epidemiology of HIV transmission among injecting and non-injecting drug users, (2) methodological training in all REA methods, and (3) operational procedures related to data handling, transfer, and general project management. In addition, teams were trained on field safety procedures and ethical standards. The training gave field team members an opportunity to practice new skills and facilitated team-building within and across sites. The training also enabled the project team to make small adjustments to procedures and instrument layout prior to entering the field.

During the training, team members from each city worked together to create preliminary maps of neighborhoods and "hotspots," locations where drug dealing, drug use, and buying and selling of drug paraphernalia was known to take place. Some sites were also identified through previous studies and site visits. These locations were used to conduct street intercepts and recruit individuals for interviews and focus groups. In addition to street intercepts, participants were also recruited through snowball sampling. During data collection, the team added new sites through a combination of mapping and observation.

Fieldwork took place over five weeks in late 2005 (see Figure 7.7). Key informant interviews explored topics such as the physical and social environment in which drugs were used; values and beliefs about drugs, and risk practices related to sex and drug use (Parry et al. 2008b). Interviews also explored perceptions about the availability of harm-reduction and treatment services and solicited recommendations. Focus groups were used mainly "to expand on, confirm, and validate" risk-related themes that emerged during interviews (Parry et al. 2008b). Participants in interviews did not take part in focus groups, and vice versa.

This project also offered free voluntary counseling and testing for HIV to all key informant interviewees, using finger prick tests and a two-step confirmatory process for those who tested positive. Persons who tested positive were referred to treatment and other services.

Analysis was conducted by MRC project staff using a qualitative data analysis software program. Site managers for each city participated in the analysis process through review of data summaries and memos and field notes.

Main findings

In all, the team conducted 131 interviews and 21 focus groups with persons who use drugs. In addition, 19 service providers also took part in 16 interviews and 1 focus group. In all, the sample included 78 persons who

Figure 7.7 Team debriefing in South Africa.

identified themselves as men who have sex with men (MSM), 115 persons involved in sex work, and 96 injecting drug users, as well as 45 participants who were non-injecting drug users and were neither MSM or sex workers. The majority of participants were men (65%), and the age range was 18–62 years of age. Of 131 key informant interviewees, 92 (70%) agreed to be tested for HIV, with 26 (28%) of them confirmed as positive. Persons testing positive were referred to HIV care and treatment services (Parry et al. 2008b).

The REA team obtained useful information about the diversity of drugs used and the most commonly used drugs across all groups and sites. The most commonly used drugs were cannabis, cocaine hydrochloride (HCL), crack cocaine, and heroin. Methaqualone, also known as Mandrax, was also used. Some inter-site differences were noted—crystal methamphetamine was more frequently reported in Cape Town, usually among MSM, while Wellconal, an analgesic, was reportedly widely used in Durban. With the exception of heroin, drug use was associated with increased sexual desire and activity. Drugs were usually smoked, but also swallowed, snorted, and injected depending on the drug.

Persons who injected drugs described participating in several practices known to increase the risk of HIV transmission, including sharing and reusing needles and syringes and failing to properly clean and dispose of used equipment. Participants described their own attempts at harm reduction such as sharing only with partners and friends, but not strangers; and attempting to sanitize needles with boiling water or lighters, none of which are effective practices for preventing transmission.

Interviews also shed light on the integration of drugs into sexual activity, describing how different drugs are used before, during, and after sex. The functional role of drugs as they relate to sexual activity was a major theme in interviews, with drugs used to provide physical energy, boost confidence, prolong sexual stamina, enhance pleasure, ease physical and psychological pain, and relax after sex work, among other functions. Many participants described polydrug use, with several different drugs used by one individual during any given time period, depending on desired function.

Participants also described the way in which drug use and sex work are intertwined socially and economically. Interviews illuminated the organization of sex work in some sites (Needle et al. 2008; Parry et al. 2009), where pimps and drug dealers facilitate drug use among sex workers and their clients and where clients often seek sex workers who will use drugs with them. Women, especially, are vulnerable to "merchants" who act as pimp, landlord, and drug dealer, providing women with shelter, drugs, and sometimes emotional benefits in exchange for income earned by women in sex work. These merchants often operate rooms or buildings that house groups of female sex workers and double as rooms used for selling drugs and sex. Female sex workers produce income for merchants in multiple ways: by buying drugs for their personal use, usually on credit; by selling sex; by soliciting drug-using clients for sex, who pay for sex and also buy drugs from the pimp; and by introducing new clients to drugs. Male pimps largely control the work and lives of female sex workers. Male sex workers, in contrast, had more autonomy over their daily lives and work schedules. They reported activity cycles of procuring and then using drugs, then selling sex to buy more drugs. These activities took place in a wider variety of venues than those frequented by women, including cars, public meeting sites, hotels, and clients' homes.

Although many participants were knowledgeable about how HIV is transmitted, there was widespread acknowledgment that drugs interfere with decision-making. Participants reported engaging in a range of sexual risk behaviors while under the influence of drugs including sex with multiple partners, having sex with strangers; taking part in "orgies" where condoms are not used, having anal sex, and submitting to unprotected sex in order to procure drugs (Parry et al. 2008a).

The REA also shed light on perceptions of health services among these populations. Although some persons who injected drugs had been tested for HIV, most participants in the REA had not been tested. Across the three sites, there was little awareness of locations for voluntary counseling and testing (VCT) for HIV and concerns about costs and loss of confidentiality. Participants also had complaints about long waits to see providers in general and stigmatizing behaviors which made them reluctant to use these and other services, such as drug treatment. Few participants were aware of the availability of treatment for HIV.

Service providers noted a lack of resources that enabled them to offer HIV testing, drug treatment, or other services that might benefit these populations. Lack of training in how to test and counsel vulnerable populations was also mentioned as a barrier.

Conclusions

The REA documented high prevalence of overlapping drug and sexual risk behaviors in all three cities that potentially contribute to the spread of HIV. Almost a third of participants were HIV positive. Sexual mixing among sub-populations, as well as sexual bridging to the broader population in South Africa was likely contributing to the epidemic in South Africa. Although many participants were aware of the potential for HIV transmission associated with high-risk drug use and sexual practices, most acknowledged that the use of drugs interfered with efforts to reduce harm. Moreover, as the REA documented, drug use was integrated socially and economically in some settings, where both sex and drugs provide income and drugs are used to enhance sex and to perpetuate further drug use (Parry et al. 2008a; Parry et al. 2008b; Parry 2009).

Numerous barriers using services were documented, including lack of substance abuse and HIV treatment services, reluctance to use services due to cost and fear of stigma, and lack of appropriate training for providers.

Recommendations

Recommendations included disseminating the results of the REA findings to target groups, stakeholders, service providers, and managers in the three cities and at the provincial and national levels (Parry et al. 2007; Parry et al. 2008b). *Advocacy* was proposed to increase resources and encourage policy changes aimed at reducing substance abuse and HIV prevalence among vulnerable drug-using populations in South Africa. *Capacity building* was suggested to strengthen and scale up community outreach to vulnerable populations and to adapt current models of HIV testing were considered priorities. The REA recommended that outreach efforts be intensified to provide education and to link affected populations to prevention, care, and treatment services. Current models of facility-based HIV counseling and testing needed adaptation to include field-based rapid testing and specific risk-reduction messaging for mobile and hard-to-reach populations. The team also recommended *integration of HIV and substance-abuse "silos"* through cross-training of HIV-prevention and substance-abuse treatment program staff, development of referral networks, and co-location of HIV testing and counseling services within substance-abuse treatment facilities.

Follow-up

The REA resulted in a "heightened response among stakeholders" (Needle et al. 2008). In 2006, a workshop held in Cape Town was attended by public and private partners, stakeholders from the three cities, researchers, and organizations that serve vulnerable populations. CDC and MRC project staff also participated. The findings from the REA were presented and a series of group discussions were held to build on preliminary recommendations in the report. In 2007 and 2008, with additional funding through PEPFAR, MRC and its partners began implementing the recommendations. Cross-training of HIV and substance-abuse treatment professionals took place and technical assistance was provided to help MRC and its partners set up linkage and referral to care systems. In Durban, a consortium of organizations working with vulnerable populations formed and began to share information and strategies for preventing HIV in these populations. In addition, the REA resulted in several published manuscripts co-authored by partners at MRC in South Africa and the CDC.

References

Needle, Richard, Karen Kroeger, Hrishikesh Belani, Angeli Achrekar, Charles D. Parry, and Sarah Dewing. 2008. Sex, drugs, and HIV: Rapid assessment of HIV risk behaviors among street-based drug-using sex workers in Durban, South Africa. *Social Science & Medicine* 67(9): 1447–1455

Parry, Charles D., Tara Carney, Petal Petersen, and Sarah Dewing. 2007. "Technical report: drug use and sexual HIV risk patterns among non-injecting and injecting drug users in Cape Town, Pretoria and Durban, South Africa." Cape Town, South Africa: Medical Research Council, Alcohol & Drug Abuse Research Unit.

Parry Charles D., Petal Petersen, Sarah Dewing, Tara Carney, Richard Needle, Karen Kroeger, and Latasha Treger L. 2008a. Rapid assessment of drug-related HIV risk among men who have sex with men in three South African cities. *Drug and Alcohol Dependency* 95(1–2): 45–53.

Parry, Charles D., Petal Petersen, Tara Carney, Sarah Dewing, and Richard Needle. 2008b. Rapid assessment of drug use and sexual HIV risk patterns among vulnerable drug-using populations in Cape Town, Durban, and Pretoria, South Africa. *SAHARA-J: Journal of Social Aspects of HIV/AIDS* 5(3): 113–119.

Parry, Charles D., Sarah Dewing, Petal Petersen, Tara Carney, Richard Needle, Karen Kroeger, and Latasha Treger. 2009. Rapid assessment of HIV risk behavior in drug using sex workers in three cities in South Africa. *AIDS and Behavior* 13(5): 849–859.

Statistics South Africa. 2006. Mid-year population estimates, South Africa. http://statssa.gov.za. Accessed February 10, 2006.

Trotter, Robert T., Richard H. Needle, Eric Goosby, Christopher Bates, and Merrill Singer. 2001. A methodological model for rapid assessment, response, and evaluation: the RARE program in public health. *Field Methods* 13(2): 137–159.

UNAIDS (Joint United Nations Programme on HIV/AIDS). 2006. *2006 Report on the Global AIDS Epidemic.* Geneva: United Nations.

Appendices

Appendix 1
Glossary of terms

Anthropology: Academic discipline that is the study of humans, human behavior, and societies.

Analysis team: A group of individuals who conduct qualitative data analysis within a REA.

Applied research: Systematic attempt to gain a better understanding of pragmatic problems or to answer specific questions, using data directly for real-world application.

Code: Labels to tag a concept or a value found in a narrative or text. Usually a word, phrase, sentence, or paragraph that is a unit of meaning that are then used to sort, group, and compare similar bits of text (or segments).

Code book: A document that contains the systematic collection of codes and their meanings.

Coding (deductive and inductive):   A key step in data analysis where labels are applied to portions or segments of data.

Conceptual framework: A model or visual representation used to illustrate and describe a phenomenon.

Confidentiality: Protecting participant information from disclosure outside the research according to the terms of the research protocol and the informed consent document.

Contract: Mechanism of funding used to procure a product or service.

Culture: The knowledge, experience, beliefs, values, attitudes, religion, and meanings that are shared by a group of people.

Data interpretation: The process of inductive reasoning to structure the meanings derived from data.

Data reduction: The process by which qualitative data is organized and structured.

Data representation: The presentation of research findings and conclusions through visual or narrative displays that represent ways of organizing, summarizing, simplifying, or transforming data.

Data sharing: The practice of making research data available to other investigators.

Debriefing: A structured REA activity through which team members share what has been learned to date and determine the direction of future data collection. Debriefing is also an opportunity to hone skills and discuss safety issues.

Decolonial: Perspective that challenges the matrix of colonial power; a set of theoretical and methodological tools that help to synthesize historical and contemporary injustice and resistance.

Deductive: In coding, refers to starting with a predefined set of codes.

Dissemination: Sharing findings and recommendations of a REA.

Emic: Categories of understanding that local people use to make sense of their world.

Etic: Categories of understanding used by researchers and "outsiders" to represent local peoples' views.

Ethnography: A qualitative method of data collection focused on studying a group of people with shared characteristics or experiences. Ethnography is based on learning from people rather than studying people, and usually draws on key-informant interviews and participant observation.

Evaluation research: A type of applied research used to measure the impact of changes in the social or physical environment. Evaluations often focus on interventions, programs, or services to determine if changes have the desired outcome.

Fieldwork: The gathering of data through interviewing and observing participants in their natural setting.

Field coordinator: A person who is designated to take the lead on managing fieldwork logistics.

Field notes: Written accounts of what is seen and heard during data collection.

Field team: In REA, an interdisciplinary group of individuals responsible for data collection.

Findings: Key information learned, summarized, and conveyed as a result of REA data collection and analysis.

Focus groups: A type of conversational interview in which a moderator facilitates a discussion among a group of people about a particular topic or topics.

Formative research: A research process that usually takes place before a program is developed or a study is conducted to help inform the design or parameters of subsequent activity. Formative research may combine qualitative and quantitative methods to help define populations, assess the potential acceptability of interventions, and identify local terminology for survey instruments, for example.

Grants: Funding provided to researchers and institutions that is meant to assist them in carrying out research.

Group interviews: In-depth interviews where of two or more people are present. Group interviews are usually impromptu and unplanned. They are different from focus group discussions, in which multiple people are invited to participate in a planned and facilitated group discussion.

Holistic: An approach that considers the entirety of a cultural system as interconnected; that takes into consideration relationships among individual-, community-, and structural-level factors.

Immersion: A "deep dive" into the data during the analysis process through reading and re-reading transcripts and field notes to become familiar with the data, debriefing with team members, and writing reflections on the data.

Inductive: In research, refers to when conclusions and hypotheses stem from the data that is collected. Hypothesis seeking rather than hypothesis testing.

Informed consent: The process of a participant understanding the risks and benefits of taking part in research and making a voluntary choice to participate.

Insiders: People who have direct experience with the problem and/or who may have insight into why certain things are occurring.

Institutional review board (IRB): Also referred to as a human subjects review board. A group formally designated to review and monitor research to ensure that the methods proposed are ethical and adhere to principles for the protections of human subjects.

Interview guide: An instrument used by the interviewer that outlines discussion topics and questions for the interview. The interview guide functions as a general guide but does not require that every question be asked in the same order.

In-depth interviews (semi-structured and structured): A qualitative data collection method that involves direct, one-on-one engagement with individual participants to explore their point of view, experiences, feelings, and perspectives in depth.

Iterative process: A process where the same steps are repeated over and over again.

Key informant: People who are able to describe and discuss key issues about their culture or the problem under investigation.

Key-informant interview: A one-on-one discussion between the researcher and a key informant.

Mapping: A method of using drawings, pictures, maps, or other types of spatial data to visually represent what is observed in the field by participants or researchers.

Member checking: A common technique used in qualitative research to ensure the accurate portrayal of participant voices by allowing participants the opportunity to confirm, clarify, or contradict the accuracy and interpretations of data.

Memoing: The act of recording reflective notes (written ideas or records about concepts and their relationships) about what the researcher is learning from the data.

Memorandum of understanding (MOU): An agreement between two or more parties that is not legally binding, but which outlines the responsibilities of each of the parties to the agreement.

Note taker: Person responsible for taking notes during interviews, during and after focus group discussions, and during observations.

Observation: Qualitative data collection method of structured seeing and listening to meet a research goal.

Participant: Individuals who are willing to participate in research through interviews, mapping, or observation and to speak about their experiences with or knowledge of a topic.

Phenomenon: The concept being studied (e.g., migration, land use, health care use).

Probes: Questions that follow-up on points that the participant makes in order for the interviewer to obtain more information.

Program assessment: A systematic method of gathering, analyzing, and using information from various sources about a program and measuring program outcomes.

Project lead: Person responsible for guiding the overall REA process, and for overseeing any approvals and funding requirements.

Qualitative data analysis software: Software programs used to manage and reduce large volumes of qualitative data. QDA helps analysts with categorizing, coding, and interpreting data.

Qualitative data management: A clear organizational system to record, manage, and account for qualitative data collected during a study.

Qualitative research: Research that focuses on learning how people make sense of their lives and experiences. Qualitative research is based on a few cases and on depth, rather than breadth. The qualitative researcher is the primary instrument for data collection and analysis and actively interacts with people, settings, sites, or institutions to observe or record behavior in its natural setting.

Rapid ethnographic assessment: An approach to data collection using primarily qualitative and ethnographic methods and interdisciplinary teams to quickly obtain information from the perspective of insiders. REAs employ principles of focused scope of inquiry, triangulation, and iterative data collection and analysis to understand emerging situations and problems.

Rapid ethnographic assessment practitioner: A person with experience conducting REAs.

Rapid response activities: A set of methods or activities to provide assistance to local areas that experience disasters, disease outbreaks, or other emergency events.

Rapport: A relationship of mutual trust and respect.

Recommendations: Statements that link REA findings with potential actions to achieve desired outcomes.

Research protocol: Description of the background, rationale, objectives, design, methodology, organization, and ethical considerations of a research project.

Sampling: Process of determining who will be included in research.

Saturation: The point in qualitative research at which no new information is being learned from interviews or focus groups.

Stakeholders: People, organizations, and institutions who have an interest in the research project or who are likely to be affected by its outcomes.

Statement of work (SOW): A written statement that clearly and succinctly lays out the work to be done in a research task or project. The SOW generally describes the scope of the work to be done and clarifies deliverables, costs, and timeline.

Street-intercept surveys: A type of brief survey often used in a REA that involves asking individuals in key locations about topics relevant to the research question. It is typically conducted where the individual is intercepted.

Team lead: In REA, the person responsible for guiding the activities of one REA team in the field, including monitoring the progress and quality of interviews, holding team debriefings, communicating with the Project Lead, and ensuring that ethical practices are adhered to by all involved.

Themes: Patterns of meaning within data that are underpinned by a central concept that organizes the analytic observations.

Transcription: Taking audio-taped data and transforming it into text for analysis.

Triangulation: The accumulation and comparison of data across multiple sources, methods, and team members to validate, confirm, and strengthen findings. In REA, multidisciplinary teams contribute to triangulation through intensive interaction, sharing of tasks, and group decision-making.

Vulnerable population: Social or demographic groups that have relatively limited access to necessary social, political, and economic resources.

Appendix 2
Sample REA concept proposal

Concept proposal title

Rapid ethnographic assessment (REA) of the HIV/STD prevention needs of sex workers in the rural Southeast

Background

Little is known about the nature and organization of female sex work or of the HIV/STD prevention needs of sex workers in the southeastern United States. Studies carried out in the 1990s in mainly large urban areas typically addressed female sex work in conjunction with drug use, particularly crack cocaine addiction (Sterk 1999). Recent strengthened enforcement of laws against human trafficking as a result of the Victims of Trafficking and Violence Prevention Act of 2000 (TVPA) has resulted in more frequent media reports of raids and arrests related to sex work, sex trafficking, and child prostitution in the Southeast; however, there is considerable conflation of sex work with sex trafficking, and reliable estimates of numbers of women in sex work or having been trafficked are lacking. In addition, most of the discussion of women trafficked into sex work has taken place from a human rights or law enforcement perspective, with little mention of the public health aspects of this issue or the specific health needs of women involved in sex work.

In addition, given recent technological advances (cell phones, internet), the nature of sex work in some areas may be rapidly changing. While HIV/STD programs have traditionally conducted outreach with street-based sex workers or relied upon jail screening programs to monitor HIV/STD prevalence among sex workers, it may be necessary to devise new strategies to address sex workers who are not street-based and who are more hidden. To date, however, there is a dearth of data on the role of technology in female sex work.

Recent studies indicate that Latino migrant men often patronize sex workers; in a study of Latino men in rural North Carolina, 32.5% of men unaccompanied by female partners and 9.5% of men with partners reported exchanging money or other goods for sex within the past three months (Knipper et al. 2007). A study of Latino day laborers in Los Angeles indicated that 26% of men had sex with a female sex worker within the past 12 months (Galvan et al. 2009). An ethnographic study carried out in three Florida agricultural towns described the context of female sex work, noting that sex workers often canvassed large areas of towns in search of clients or traveled to farm worker camps to solicit men who lacked transportation (Bletzer 2003). Recent anecdotal reports from North Carolina, Florida, and Georgia indicate that female sex workers who serve Hispanic migrant men may be highly mobile in the Southeast, moving of their own volition, or being transported by other agents; however, to date there appears to have been few if any data systematically collected on this issue.

Purpose and objectives

The purpose of this REA is to gather exploratory data on the organization and typology of sex work in select locations, including patterns of mobility among sex workers, with a particular focus on sex workers who serve Latino men. Data will be gathered through key-informant interviews with individuals from local health, social service, and advocacy organizations that have contact with or knowledge of sex workers. Field observations and mapping of relevant sites will also be conducted to create a "snapshot" of the nature of sex work in the area and to get a better understanding of the context in which sex work activities are being carried out. The assessment will address the following questions:

- What is the current organization and typology of female sex work in a defined area?
- Who are the predominant clientele being served by female sex workers in various settings?
- What are the current patterns of mobility among sex workers and their clients?
- What is the need for and availability of HIV/STD prevention and other supportive services for sex workers and their clients?

The REA will help to inform the public health response to the HIV/STD prevention needs of sex workers and their clients by:

- Identifying locations and venues where sex work takes place
- Identifying patterns in behavior that potentially contribute to HIV/STD risk and transmission among sex workers and their clients
- Identifying gaps in services for sex workers and their clients
- Identifying opportunities for HIV/STD programs to collaborate or coordinate with partners who provide services to sex workers and their clients, including services to women who may have been trafficked.

Methods and analysis

The REA is a collaboration between the CDC and the North Carolina HIV/STD Prevention and Care Program. The REA will be carried out by a four-person team using a team-based approach to rapid collection and analysis of qualitative data gathered through interviews, observations, and mapping. Key-informant interviews will be carried out with providers from community health facilities, state- and county-level HIV/STD programs, and community-based organizations working with immigrant and refugee populations and with trafficked women, among others. An initial list of contacts will be generated through discussions with the North Carolina state and local HIV/STD programs. Prior to traveling to the field site, the field team will conduct planning conference calls with state partners and informational calls with local community-based and social service organizations to determine the appropriate contacts, set up appointments, and identify relevant locations for observations. The list of key informants will be expanded through chain referral during fieldwork activities. Data collection is estimated to take five working days. CDC will prepare a protocol and interview guide with topical domains in advance for review and comment. CDC will also handle obtaining necessary human subjects approvals for the final protocol. Analysis of interview, observation and mapping data will be carried out by the REA team and a report of findings with recommendations will be prepared for the state HIV/STD Program. The draft of the written report will be circulated to the state for discussion prior to finalizing.

References

Bletzer, Keith. 2003. Risk and danger among women-who-prostitute in areas where farmworkers predominate. *Medical Anthropology Quarterly* 17(2): 251–278.

Galvan, Frank H., Daniel J. Ortiz, Victor Martinez, and Eric G. Bing. 2009. The use of female commercial sex workers' services by Latino day laborers. *Hispanic Journal of Behavioral Sciences* 31(4): 553–575.

Knipper, Emily, Scott D. Rhodes, Kristen Lindstrom, Fred R. Bloom, Jami S. Leichliter, and Jaime Montaño. 2007. Condom use among heterosexual immigrant Latino men in the southeastern United States. *AIDS Education and Prevention* 19(5): 436–447.

Sterk, Claire E. 1999. *Fast Lives: Women Who Use Crack Cocaine*. Philadelphia: Temple University Press.

Appendix 3
Sample project planning tool

Task	Person/s Responsible	Comments/Notes	Target Completion Date	Date Completed
Protocol Development and Approval				
Draft protocol submitted to [funder, program] for review and changes				
Changes incorporated into final protocol				
Final protocol submitted to IRB for human subjects review				
Protocol approved				
Budget				
Develop budget				
Budget submitted and approved				
Training Preparation				
REA training dates selected				
REA training curriculum and materials developed				
Training site located and reserved				
Finalize training participant list and send letters of invitation				
Arrange per diem or transport for participants				

(*Continued*)

Task	Person/s Responsible	Comments/Notes	Target Completion Date	Date Completed
Prepare all training materials (print manuals, obtain audio-video/DVD equipment, pens, markers, flip charts, certificates of completion)		Determine if sub-contract needed for materials development or procurement		
Develop/update evaluation tool for training				
Obtain computers for analysis training		Depends on analysis plan		
Establish regular call schedule for fieldwork and training prep		Will need weekly calls to discuss progress and training plans		
Fieldwork Preparation				
Site visit to cities where REA will be conducted		Reach out to local CBOs/NGOs to arrange meeting times		
Identify local recruiting locations				
Identify and rent field office locations		Team will need convenient location for debriefing, meetings, materials storage, etc.		
Identify sites for interviews and focus groups		Must be private and quiet		
Identify preliminary sites for observations, mapping, street intercepts		Obtain any necessary approvals		
Inform local officials and security about study and obtain letters of authorization if needed				
Organize and compile field supplies		Need T shirts, badges, bags for equipment, operational manual, recorders?		
Develop Operational Manual for interviewers: (written logs and procedures, letters of authorization, interview guides, protocols, data collection forms, etc.)				

Task	Person/s Responsible	Comments/Notes	Target Completion Date	Date Completed
Arrange drinks/snacks for focus groups				
Select and order recording equipment		Will need one for each team of interviewers		
Select and order laptops for field		Will need one per site		
Train staff to use recorders		Can be part of methods training or separate but will need to train staff		
Data handling/security and management plan developed		Procedures for transfer and security of data files, recorders		
Staffing				
Create job descriptions for field team members and coordinators as needed				
Field team members selected and hired		Need four field teams per site (two-person teams)		
Data transcribing service selected				
Analysis team identified				
Develop data analysis plan				
Identify service to transcribe recordings				
Develop data management plan (handling, security, monitoring)				
Identify analysis team lead and members				
Dissemination Plan				
Develop plan for dissemination of findings (final report, meetings, etc.)				

Appendix 4

Sample REA budget template

Summary Proposal Budget					Budget Justification
Project Title: **Project Period:** **Project Lead:** **Submitting organization:**					
	Name	**An Sal**	**% Effort**		
Personnel:					
Project/Team Lead		$81,000	10%	$8,100	To conduct fieldwork, data collection and analysis, report writing
Field Coordinator		$62,000	10%	$6,200	
Total:				**$14,300**	
	$ /hour	**# of Hrs**	**# of Wks**		
Team members (4)	19.00	40	6	$18,240	To conduct fieldwork, data collection and analysis, report writing
Total:				**$18,240**	
Fringe Benefits	8.0%			$2,603	
Total:				**$2,603**	
Total Salaries & Fringe:				**$35,143**	
Equipment:					
Laptop (4)				$4,000	
Digital recorders (4)				$1,000	
Total:				**$5,000**	

Summary Proposal Budget					Budget Justification
Project Title:					
Project Period:					
Project Lead:					
Submitting organization:					
	Name	**An Sal**	**% Effort**		
Travel and Hotel					
Domestic				$10,000	Travel to and from field site during fieldwork and any necessary follow-up
Foreign					
Total Travel:				**$10,000**	
Other Direct Costs:					
Participant tokens of appreciation				$250	
Materials & Supplies				$250	
Printing costs				$250	Printing related to data collection
Software purchase				$1,000	
Transcription				$1,000	
Rent: 5 days × $100				$500	Interview/ location
Phone/Internet				$250	
Other				$500	
Total:				**$4,000**	
TOTAL DIRECT COSTS:				**$54,143**	
FACILITIES & ADMINISTRATIVE COSTS:	52.0%			**$21,397**	
TOTAL PROJECT COSTS:				**$75,540**	

Appendix 5
Sample REA team position descriptions

Project Lead

- Guides the overall REA process
- Leads the development of the REA protocol
- Communicates REA goals and objectives to stakeholders
- Explains REA methods and the benefit and value of the REA approach to stakeholders
- Oversees any approvals and funding requirements
- Ensures team members are selected based on REA criteria
- Coordinates methods and analysis training for REA team members
- Conducts and leads meetings with stakeholders

Team Lead

- Aids in the development of the REA protocol
- Guides activities of one REA team in the field
- Monitors the conduct of interviews
- Ensures that ethical practices are adhered to by team members
- Collaborates with fellow team members to carry out the work
- Assigns interviews to team members based on content expertise or other factors
- Communicates with the Project Lead about the project
- Makes implementation decisions when appropriate
- Leads team debriefings

Field Coordinator

- Coordinates fieldwork logistics and mapping
- Set ups and manages the fieldwork calendar
- Schedules interviews to allow for transportation time between sites
- Prepares a preliminary schedule to share with the team
- Coordinates meetings with stakeholders
- Communicates with Project and Team Leads about the project

REA Team Members

- Aid in the development of the REA protocol
- Participate in REA training
- Perform data collection tasks
- Take part in debriefing sessions
- Conduct data analysis if necessary
- Help write up final report and present findings

Appendix 6
Sample statement of work

Title

Transcription and Translation Support for Project: [*HIV Risk in Sex Workers in Country X*].

Background

This statement of work addresses qualitative data analysis support for the [Project Name] project. The purpose of the project is to assess HIV risk and the need for public health interventions and services among vulnerable populations. Technical work of the project will be carried out by [Organization name] and its partners.

[Country X] is facing a severe, generalized HIV/AIDS epidemic. A REA is being carried out to better understand, assess, and make recommendations to address the needs of vulnerable populations in three cities. The assessment will explore the context of high-risk sexual behavior among female sex workers and their male sex partners. The possibility of increased HIV risk creates the need for targeted prevention programming and improved access to services for these populations.

Description/Purpose of contract

The purpose of this contract is to provide transcription and translation support for the project and its partners. Tasks include preparation of approximately 130 English-language interview transcripts for purposes of qualitative data analysis.

Statement of work

The Contractor will furnish all necessary personnel, materials, services, and facilities incidental to the performance of the work as stated in this contract. The main activities needed to support the project are described below.

Transcription tasks

- Transcribe and prepare 130 digitally recorded English-language interview transcripts.

  o Key-informant interviews: 100 interviews × 1 hour in length = 100 hours
  o Focus group interviews: 30 interviews × 1.5 hours in length = 45 hours
  o Total hours of interviews to be transcribed = 145 hours

- Prepare transcripts using the transcription conventions described in the approved study protocol.
- Prepare transcripts that provide a verbatim record of the interview, including slang or colloquial terminology, as used by the interviewer and participants.
- Accurately label all transcripts according to the instructions provided by the study team (interview code/number, site, interview date, interviewer, transcriber, date transcribed, etc.)
- Prepare single-spaced, typed transcripts in 12 pt. Arial font, with 1-inch margins and numbered pages, and make them available in electronic format.
- Persons transcribing should be fluent in English.
- Randomly audit (with the study team) selected transcripts for accuracy.
- Maintain a log of work received and work completed and deliver transcripts according to an agreed-upon schedule. This may involve preparing batches of some categories of interviews before others in order to facilitate the analysis process.
- Meet with the Project Lead (or other appropriate person) on a weekly or bi-weekly basis to discuss progress and any problems that need to be addressed.
- Participate in scheduled phone calls with technical teams to discuss progress in the project.
- Deliverables: 130 transcripts, as described above, within 30 days of receipt of digital recordings.

Appendix 7

Interview guide template

Interview # or code: _____   Date: _____
Person interviewed: _____   Interviewer: _____
Location: _____ Note taker: _____

Introduction

Begin the interview by making a short statement that explains the purpose of the interview and lets the participant know that his or her views are valued. Let the person know about how much time the interview will take. Let the person know that what they say—any comments they make—will not be connected to their name. Let them know if you are recording and how. Ask the person if they have any questions before beginning the interview. This lets the participant know what to expect and what the guidelines are for taking part in the interview.

Example:
We are trying to get a better understanding of the nature of sex work in this area. Recently, we've heard some anecdotal reports about sex workers who serve male clients in the Southeast, including North Carolina. Some of these reports have been about sex workers who may be mobile or who may be serving mobile migrant men. We are trying to learn more about this issue, and we feel that your thoughts and experiences may be helpful. We'd like to understand more about the kind of sex work that goes on this area, and about the kinds of health and social services that are currently available to sex workers. We'd like to know what kinds of services may be needed.

Thank you for taking the time to participate in this interview. The interview should take about 45–60 minutes. At the end of the interview you will be able to ask any questions that are of interest to you. The information you give us may be used in a report; however, your name will not appear in the report and it will not be connected to any comments you make. We are taking written notes of what you say, but we are not recording the interview.

Do you have any questions before we begin?
Do you agree to take part in the interview?

Demographics or background information

Most interviews will include a brief list of questions that help the interviewer know more about the person being interviewed. These can include such items as age, race, gender, ethnicity, or other relevant items. Items such as job title can be important in terms of the perspectives being shared. This information also will help summarize and describe who the participants were.

Example:
To start with, I have a few basic questions that I'd like for you to answer:

- What is your current position/job title?
    - How long have you been in this position?
    - What do you consider your primary responsibilities?
    - What services does your agency provide?

Grand-tour question

The purpose of this section is to solicit the participant's point of view without influence of the interviewer or of the focused questions that follow. It is one of the most important elements of the interview because it allows for the discovery of unanticipated areas of concern for community members and providers. It provides a forum for them to disclose their agenda up front. It is most important that the interviewer does not lead the participant in any way, though encouragement is sometimes needed. If necessary, encourage the participant by repeating elements of the above statements or very general probes (e.g., "I just want to know what you think." "Tell me more about that." etc.)

The interviewer may also use silence as a probe. To do this, you will need to be comfortable with silence. With someone having difficulty, you might start by saying "Take your time and think for a while—just tell me what your thoughts are." Avoid interrupting the participant while they are speaking.

Example:
Now, I'd like to move onto our main topic: sex work
What can you tell us about sex work in this area? What are your thoughts?
Please feel free to discuss whatever you think is important about this topic. Some people find this difficult but I'd like you to try your best. Usually it gets easier once you get started. So, how would you describe sex work in this area? In terms of who is involved, where it takes place, anything at all.

The interviewer can also try asking: "What do you think is important for us to know?" Asking this question after the participant has shared their initial thoughts can sometimes open up new lines of inquiry or help the participant elaborate on what they have just shared.

Main body of interview

The interview guide should be constructed with a set of open-ended questions that relate to the topic. The guide is just that—it sets the broad parameters of the interview in terms of what the interviewer is trying to learn but is open and flexible enough to accommodate new and relevant information. The questions will not necessarily be asked in the order printed in the guide, but the interviewer uses the guide as a kind of checklist to help keep the interview on track. The guide can also include probes and tips for the interviewer to help them remember the kind of information that would be of interest.

> Example:
> What can you tell me about the kinds of sex work that goes on around here? Can you tell me what you have heard about this?

Here we are trying to describe the typology of sex work from the participant's perspective—how they might categorize different types of sex work. For example, this could be based upon different types of women who engage in sex work, location where sex work takes place, clientele, type of services provided, etc. Let the participant determine this.

> Example:
> Can you describe for me some of the women you run into during your outreach work who are involved in sex work?

> PROBE:
>> How old would you say most of them are?
>> Where would you say they are coming from?

The guide should use open-ended questions and questions that will elicit description and detail. The interviewer is seeking to start a conversation about a topic and would like more information.

> Example:
> How do sex workers and their male clients find each other? What are the various means they use?

> PROBE:

> - How do the sex workers advertise their services? Where?
> - How do they make contact? Do they use mobile phones?
> - Are there handlers or pimps involved?

At appropriate intervals, the interviewer may need to segue into the next part of the interview. This can be signaled to the participant in a conversational manner.

> Example:
> I really appreciate you sharing your views on sex work. Now I'd like to turn to another topic—I'd like to talk about the kinds of health services that may be needed.
> Based on your experience, what kind of HIV/STD prevention services are needed in this area for sex workers and their clients?
> What would a successful program to address the needs of women involved in sex work look like?
> PROBE: What do you think the priorities should be?

In general, it is good practice to limit the guide to 10–15 well-crafted, open-ended questions for a 60-minute interview, but there is no hard and fast rule. The number of questions depends on the topic, and the way questions are framed. The answer to a later question may be answered early on, eliminating the need to ask it in order. The most important point is that the interview is not rushed or formulaic and that participants have time to be thoughtful about their answers.

Wrap up questions

It can be useful to signal the end of the interview and give the participant one last chance to add anything.

> Example:
> Thank you again talking with me. We're coming to the end of the interview, but I have a few more questions to ask before we close.
> First, is there anything else you think we should know about this topic?

If using chain referral, remember to ask the participant for other names.

> Example:
> Who else should I talk to in order to learn more about these issues?

List names and contact info.
   May we tell them that you have referred us to them?

Closing and follow-up

Clarify any follow-up.

> Example:
> May we contact you again for further information or clarification of responses?

YES NO (circle one)
Remember to ask if there are any questions at the close of the interview.

Example:
Do you have any other questions?
If there are materials to be distributed (e.g., brochures, referral cards), be sure to hand these to the participant.
Quite often, participants will ask what comes after the REA—will they hear about the results, learn about the recommendations put forth, etc. Have a simple but accurate answer ready. Do not overpromise or commit to things you have no control over.

Example:
The analysis of our data will take several weeks. We will write a report, along with recommendations, and that report will be provided to the state. We anticipate that the final report will be delivered to the state in about four months. We always encourage the state to share the findings more broadly with the local community, and we hope that will be the case here.

Thank you again for your time.

Appendix 8
Interview note-taking guide

- Write and type verbatim as much as possible what people actually say. Do not just summarize what they said. Use complete sentences as much as possible. Try not to use bullet points.
- Attempt to capture terminology or slang used. Write: "working the pouches" (Health Department Communicable Disease Specialist term for working active syphilis cases).
- Put powerful or memorable quotes in quotation marks to indicate that these are direct quotes: "The budget cuts have been brutal. People are dying."
- Avoid putting your own interpretation of things or drawing conclusions in your notes. Avoid making statements such as "The participant seems to hate her clients." Instead, show what the participant did or said that demonstrates this. Write: The participant referred to her clients as "idiots" and said, "The way they behave, we shouldn't spend our state's money on them. They don't deserve it."
- You can and should, however, make observations about what you see and hear. Put these in brackets, e.g., [Participant made disparaging comments about clients—she referred to them several times as "stupid"].
- Do include your own observations of the participant's behaviors and emotions. Put your observations in brackets. Write: [The participant started to weep uncontrollably at this point] or [The participant became very animated when talking about the work she does].
- Do make notes on things you missed or things you want to remember or follow up on, e.g., [She said something about running out of bicillin—we need to follow up on this].
- Refer to interview subjects as "participants," not "respondents." (This saves time later when writing things up.)
- Do make separate notes on other things you see in the environment, e.g., [All the chairs in the waiting room were completely full and there were about ten people sitting on the floor.]

Appendix 9
Sample REA training agenda

Day 1					
Time	*Minutes*	*Topic*	*Activities*	*Objectives*	*Materials*
9:00–9:30	30	**Welcome & Introduction**	• Welcome • Introductions • Overview curriculum	• Intro group and trainers	• Flip chart for Q's
9:30–10:30	60	**Overview REA**	• Presentation (45) • Discussion (15)		• Slides
10:30–10:45	15	**Break**			
10:45–11:15	30	**Overview of Project**			• Content and background slides
11:15–12:15	60	**Methods: Mapping and Observations**	• Presentation (40) • Activity 1: Observation (20)	• Learn observation skills • Engage participants • Learn about mapping	• Part 2 slides • Observation handout • YouTube video: Japan • Audio speakers/ internet connection • Pens/ paper
12:15–1:15	60	**Lunch**			
1:15–2:45	90/105	**Methods: Key-Informant Interviews**	• Activity 2: Intro Facilitator role play (15) • Presentation (30) • Activity 3: Practice interviewing (60) (groups of 3: Interviewer, respondent, note taker)	• Demonstrate interviewing techniques • Practice interviewing skills (probe/consent) • Receive feedback on skills	• Interviewer: Trainer • Respondent: Assistant • Activity 2 guide: "Most memorable vacation?" • Slides • Activity 3 Interview guide

Day 1					
Time	*Minutes*	*Topic*	*Activities*	*Objectives*	*Materials*
2:45–3:00	15	**Break**			
3:00–4:00	60	**Workshop the Interview Guide**	• Activity 4: Workshop the guide (60)	• Clarify questions and identify possible issues with guide	• Scribe • Project interview guide
4:00–4:30	30	**Wrap up**	• Summary • Q&A		

Day 2					
Time	*Minutes*	*Topic*	*Activities*	*Objectives*	*Materials*
9:00–9:15	15	**Welcome & Recap**	• Welcome (5) • Recap key points (5) • Overview curriculum (5)		• Flip Chart
9:15–9:45	30	**Personal experience with REA**			• Slides
9:45–10:45	60	**Writing & Expanding Field Notes**	• Presentation • Activity 5: Facilitators demonstrate scripted interview • Discussion	• Practice taking field notes • Practice expanding notes with team • Identify what information was missed and identify strategies for field	• Use transcript for interview • Interviewer: • Respondent: • Notebook/ pens
10:45–11:00	15	**Break**			
11:00–12:00	60	**Debriefing**	• Presentation • Activity 6: Debriefing tips • Discussion	• Increase debriefing skills • Become familiar with templates	• Handout • Debriefing guide/ templates
12:00–1:00	60	**Lunch**			
1:00–1:45	45	**Principles of Analysis and Reporting Out**		• Analysis principles • Coding • Reporting/ concrete recommendations • Linking findings to recommendations	

(Continued)

Day 2					
Time	*Minutes*	*Topic*	*Activities*	*Objectives*	*Materials*
1:45–2:45	60	**Practice Interviewing**	• Activity 3: Practice Interviewing (60) • (Groups of 3: Interviewer, respondent, note taker/ observer)	• Consent • Go over guide • Practice skills	• Interview Guide • Trainers provide feedback
2:45–3:00	15	**Break**			
3:00–3:45	45	**Project Operations and Procedures**		• Data management • Type notes • Turning in notes process	• Guides • Calendar • Debriefing guide • Team Logistic sheet
3:45–4:30	45	**Wrap up**	• Summary • Q&A • Evaluation		

Appendix 10
Sample training budget

Category	Quantity	Price	Total price
Printing			
Participant's manual	55	30.00	1,650.00
Trainers manual	5	15.00	75.00
Interview guide, evaluation tool, exercises tool	55	15.00	825.00
Travel			
Participant airfare	15	500.00	7,500.00
Participant local travel (taxi)	15	50.00	750.00
Hotel			
15 participants × 5 nights	75	100.00	7,500.00
4 trainers × 6 nights	24	100.00	2,400.00
Facilitators			
Contracts for facilitators	5	100.00	500.00
Venue for training			
Room (1 big) × 5 days	5	200.00	1,000.00
Rooms (2 small) × 5 days	10	150.00	1,500.00
Room (1 small) × 5 days	5	150.00	750.00
Meals			
Coffee breaks + lunches for participants	1	2,000.00	2,000.00
Supplies			
General office supplies (notebooks, pens, pencils, erasers, sharpers, flipcharts, pen markers, etc.)	1	1,000.00	1,000.00
Bags for participants	60	15.00	900.00
Budget Total			28,350.00

Appendix 11
Sample REA report template

Background and purpose of the assessment

- Provide a brief review of the current data and literature related to the problem.
- Lay out the purpose of the REA—what it was supposed to accomplish.

Design and methods

- Provide a brief description of REA methods and explain the rationale for using this method for this particular research or problem.
- Describe where and when the REA took place.
- Describe who was interviewed and how they were recruited.
- Describe how the REA was supported technically and financially.
- Mention the necessary human subjects approvals that were obtained.
- Describe how local staff or stakeholders were engaged.
- Describe who was on the REA team, their disciplinary training, and their roles in various REA tasks.
- Describe all main fieldwork procedures, including the conduct of interviews (consent, note taking or recording, tokens of appreciation), observations, field notes, debriefing.
- Describe the analysis and writing, including the analytic procedures, who participated in analysis, and report writing.

Findings

- Describe the participants as a group, including any demographics, important role categories, etc.
- Describe how many interviews were conducted and where in general they took place.
- Describe in detail other fieldwork methods conducted such as observations, brief surveys, and mapping.
- Describe what was learned in terms of main themes and findings. Present these in an organized fashion, as this is the narrative "meat" of the report.

Organize content around themes and interpretations, providing evidence for the interpretations. Be sure it addresses or answers the main research questions. When writing, always refer back to the questions the REA was meant to answer—not everything that was learned will be relevant. Focus on the main questions and how the REA informed these.

Discussion and conclusions

- Provide a brief summary review of the main findings (but don't repeat everything in the previous section).
- State the main conclusions based on findings, and their implications for the program or the problem (e.g., What are the public health implications of what was learned?).

Limitations

- Acknowledge and be clear about the limitations of REA in general and this one in particular while also being clear about the benefits and usefulness of the work conducted.

Recommendations

- Provide recommendations—work toward a set of actionable and specific recommendations that link to your report findings and conclusions. Recommendations can be presented in narrative or table form.

References

- Includes a list of relevant references.

Appendices

- Interview guide.
- List of participating organizations and contact information. Be careful about confidentiality issues. In many REAs, who participates is often known, but specifically what they said is protected. The benefit of providing a list of participating organizations with names and contact information is that these organizations are often working on the issue being assessed and are likely to be involved in any follow-up. The list can be useful for networking, planning stakeholder forums, and other collaborative efforts.

Appendix 12
Rapid ethnographic assessment resources

Articles and books about REA methods

Ackerman, Sara, Nathaniel Gleason, and Ralph Gonzalez. 2015. Using rapid ethnography to support the design and implementation of health information technologies. *Studies in Health Technology and Informatics* 215: 14–27.

Beebe, James. 1995. Basic concepts and techniques of rapid appraisal. *Human Organization* 54(1): 42–51.

Beebe, James 2014. *Rapid Qualitative Inquiry: A Field Guide to Team-Based Assessment*. Lanham, MD: Rowman and Littlefield

Chambers, Robert. 1981. Rapid rural appraisal: Rationale and repertoire. *Public Administration and Development* 1(2): 95–106.

Manderson, Lenore and Peter Aab. 1992. An epidemic in the field? Rapid assessment procedures and health research. *Social Science & Medicine* 34(7): 839–850.

McNall, Miles and Pennie G. Foster-Fishman. 2007. Methods of rapid evaluation, assessment, and appraisal. *American Journal of Evaluation* 28(2): 151–168.

Trotter, Richard T., and Merrill Singer. 2005. Rapid assessment strategies for public health: Promise and problems. In *Community Interventions and AIDS*. Edited by Edison J. Trickett and Willo Pequegnat, 130–152. New York: Oxford University Press.

Trotter, Richard T., Richard H. Needle, Eric Goosby, Christopher Bates, and Merrill A. Singer. 2001. A methodological model for rapid assessment, response and evaluation: The RARE program in public health. *Field Methods* 13(2):137–159.

Utarini, Ada, Anna Winkvist, and Gretel Pelto. 2001. Appraising studies in health using rapid assessment procedures (RAP): Eleven critical criteria. *Human Organization* 60(4): 390–400.

Vindrola-Padros, Cecilia and Bruno Vindrola-Padros. 2018. Quick and dirty? A systematic review of the use of rapid ethnographies in healthcare organisation and delivery. *BMJ Quality and Safety* 27(4): 321–330.

Specific studies using REA

Bentley, Margaret E., Gretel H. Pelto, Walter L. Straus, Debra A. Schumann, Catherine Adegbola, Emanuela de la Pena, Gbolohan A. Oni, Kenneth H. Brown, and Sandra L. Huffman. 1988. Rapid ethnographic assessment: Applications in a diarrhea management program. *Social Science & Medicine* 27(1): 107–116.

Bloom, Frederick R., Kata Chillag, and Mary Yetter. 2003. Philadelphia's syphilis outbreak in gay men: An application of rapid ethnographic assessment for public health in the US. *Practicing Anthropology* 25(4): 28–32.

Brown, David Richard, Agueda Hernández, Gilbert Saint-Jean, Siân Evans, Ida Tafari, Luther G. Brewster, Michel J. Celestin et al. 2008. A participatory action research pilot study of urban health disparities using rapid assessment response and evaluation. *American Journal of Public Health* 98(1): 28–38.

Burks, Derek J., Rockey Robbins, and Jayson P. Durtschi. 2001. American Indian gay, bisexual and two-spirit men: A rapid assessment of HIV/AIDS risk factors, barriers to prevention and culturally-sensitive intervention. *Culture, Health & Sexuality* 13(3): 283–298.

Burrows, Dave, Franz Trautmann, Lizz Frost, Murdo Bijl, Yuri Sarankov, Anya Sarang, and Oksana Chernenko. 2000. Processes and outcomes of training on rapid assessment and response methods on injecting drug use and related HIV infection in the Russian Federation. *International Journal of Drug Policy* 11(1–2): 151–167.

Charlesworth, Sara and Donna Baines. 2015. Understanding the negotiation of paid and unpaid care work in community services in cross-national perspective: The contribution of a rapid ethnographic approach. *Journal of Family Studies* 21(1): 7–21.

Coreil, Jeannine, Antoine Augustin, Elizabeth Holt, and Neal A. Halsey. 1989. Use of ethnographic research for instrument development in a case-control study of immunization use in Haiti. *International Journal of Epidemiology* 18(4 Suppl 2): S33–S37.

Dorabjee, Jimmy and Luke Samson. 2000. A multi-centre rapid assessment of injecting drug use in India. *International Journal of Drug Policy* 11(1–2): 99–112.

Ezard, Nadine, Edna Oppenheimer, Ann Burton, Marian Schilperoord, David Macdonald, Moruf Adelekan, Abandokoth Sakarati, and Mark van Ommeren. 2011. Six rapid assessments of alcohol and other substance use in populations displaced by conflict. *Conflict and Health* 5(1):1.

Goepp, Julius G., Simon Meykler, Nancy E. Mooney, Claudia Lyon, Rosanne Raso, and Kell Julliard. 2008. Provider insights about palliative care barriers and facilitators: Results of a rapid ethnographic assessment. *American Journal of Hospice and Palliative Medicine* 25(4): 309–314.

Hanckel Benjamin, Danny Ruta, Gwenda Scott, Janet L. Peacock, and Judith Green. 2019. The Daily Mile as a public health intervention: A rapid ethnographic assessment of uptake and implementation in South London, UK. *BMC Public Health* 19(1): 1–167.

Hardy, Lisa Jane, Kyle D. Bohan, and Robert T. Trotter II. 2013. Synthesizing evidence based strategies and community engaged research: A model to address social determinants of health. *Public Health Reports* 128(Suppl 3): 68–76.

Kumar, M. Suresh, Shakuntala Mudaliar, S. P. Thyagarajan, Senthil Kumar, Arun Selvanayagam, and Desmond Daniels. 2000. Rapid assessment and response to injecting drug use in Madras, South India. *International Journal of Drug Policy* 11(1–2): 83–98.

Low, Setha M., Dana H. Taplin, and Mike Lamb. 2005. Battery Park City: An ethnographic field study of the community impact of 9/11. *Urban Affairs Review* 40(5): 655–682.

Mignone, Javier, G. M. Hiremath, Venkatesh Sabnis, J. Laxmi, Shiva Halli, John O'Neil, B. M. Ramesh, James Blanchard, and Stephen Moses. 2009. Use of rapid ethnographic methodology to develop a village-level rapid assessment tool predictive of HIV infection in rural India. *International Journal of Qualitative Methods* 8(3): 52–67.

Morzaria-Luna, Hem Nalini, Peggy Turk-Boyer, and Marcia Moreno-Baez. 2014. Social indicators of vulnerability for fishing communities in the Northern Gulf of California, Mexico: implications for climate change. *Marine Policy* 45: 182–193.

Needle, Richard, Karen Kroeger, Hrishikesh Belani, Angeli Achrekar, Charles D. Parry, and Sarah Dewing. 2008. Sex, drugs, and HIV: rapid assessment of HIV risk behaviors among street-based drug using sex workers in Durban, South Africa. *Social Science & Medicine* 67(9): 1447–1455.

Needle, Richard H., Robert T. Trotter, Merrill Singer, Christopher Bates, J. Bryan Page, David Metzger, and Louis H. Marcelin. 2003. Rapid assessment of the HIV/AIDS crisis in racial and ethnic minority communities: an approach for timely community interventions. *American Journal of Public Health* 93(6): 970–979.

Poteat, Tonia, Daouda Diouf, Fatou Maria Drame, Marieme Ndaw, Cheikh Traore, Mandeep Dhaliwal, Chris Beyrer, and Stefan Baral. 2011. HIV risk among MSM in Senegal: A qualitative rapid assessment of the impact of enforcing laws that criminalize same sex practices. *PloS ONE* 6(12): e28760.

Reid, Joan A. 2013. Rapid assessment exploring impediments to successful prosecutions of sex traffickers of US minors. *Journal of Police and Criminal Psychology* 28(1): 75–89.

Sabin, Miriam, George Luber, Keith Sabin, Mayte Paredes, and Edgar Monterroso. 2008. Rapid ethnographic assessment of HIV/AIDS among Garífuna communities in Honduras: Informing HIV surveillance among Garífuna women. *Journal of Human Behavior in the Social Environment* 17(3–4): 237–257.

Saleem, Jason J., William R. Plew, Ross C. Speir, Jennifer Herout, Nancy R. Wilck, Dale Marie Ryan, Theresa A. Cullen, Jean M. Scott, Murielle S. Beene, and Toni Phillips. 2015. Understanding barriers and facilitators to the use of clinical information systems for intensive care units and anesthesia record keeping: A rapid ethnography. *International Journal of Medical Informatics* 84 (7): 500–511.

Schwitters, Amee, Philip Lederer, Leah Zilversmit, Paula Samo Gudo, Isaias Ramiro, Luisa Cumba, Epifano Mahagaja, and Kebba Jobarteh. 2015. Barriers to health care in rural Mozambique: A rapid ethnographic assessment of planned mobile health clinics for ART. *Global Health Science and Practice* 3(1): 109–116.

Siri, Pablo and Silvia Inchaurraga. 2000. 'First steps': Using rapid assessment and response methods to develop research, intervention and advocacy capacity for addressing drug use in Rosario City, Argentina. *International Journal of Drug Policy* 11(1–2): 125–132.

Taplin, Dana H., Suzanne Scheld, and Setha M. Low. 2002. Rapid ethnographic assessment in urban parks: A case study of Independence National Historical Park. *Human Organization* 61(1): 80–93.

Westphal, Lynne M., and Jennifer L. Hirsch. 2010. Engaging Chicago residents in climate change action: Results from rapid ethnographic inquiry. *Cities and the Environment (CATE)* 3(1): 13.

REA field guides and toolkits

Gittelson, Joel, Pertti J. Pelto, Margaret J. Bentley, Karabi Bhattacharyya, and Joan L. Jensen. 1998. *Rapid Assessment Procedures (RAP) — Ethnographic Methods to Investigate Women's Health*. Boston, MA: International Nutrition Foundation. Accessed October 25, 2019. http://archive.unu.edu/unupress/food2/UIN01E/UIN01E00.HTM

Scrimshaw, Nevin and Gary Gleason. 1992. *Rapid Assessment Procedures: Qualitative Methodologies for Planning and Evaluation of Health Related Programs*. Boston, MA: International Nutrition Foundation for Developing Countries. Accessed October 25, 2019. www.unu.edu/unupress/food2/UIN08E/uin08e00.htm

United Nations High Commission on Refugees (UNHCR) & World Health Organization (WHO). 2008. *Rapid Assessment of Alcohol and Other Substance Use in Conflict Affected Situations: A Field Guide*. Geneva: United Nations High Commission on Refugees. Accessed October 29, 2019. https://www.who.int/mental_health/publications/field_guide_alcohol_substance_use/en/

World Health Organization (WHO). 2001. *HIV/AIDS Rapid Assessment Guide*. Geneva: World Health Organization. Accessed October 28, 2019. https://www.who.int/hiv/topics/vct/sw_toolkit/hiv_aids_rapid_assessment_guide.pdf

World Health Organization (WHO). 2002. *HIV/AIDS sex work toolkit*. Geneva: World Health Organization. Accessed October 25, 2019. https://www.who.int/hiv/topics/vct/sw_toolkit/en/

World Health Organization (WHO). 2002. *SEX-RAR (Rapid Assessment and Response) Guide: The Rapid Assessment and Response Guide on Psychoactive Substance Use and Sexual Risk Behaviour*. Geneva: World Health Organization. Accessed October 25, 2019. https://www.who.int/hiv/topics/vct/sw_toolkit/121substancesexrar.pdf

Articles on methods and analysis

Analysis

Burgess-Allen, Jilla and Vicki Owen-Smith. 2010. Using mind mapping techniques for rapid qualitative data analysis in public participation processes. *Health Expectations* 13(4):406–415.

Hannah, David R., and Brenda A. Lautsch. 2011. Counting in qualitative research: Why to conduct it, when to avoid it, and when to closet it. *Journal of Management Inquiry* 20(1): 14–22.

Ryan, Gery W., and Russell Bernard. 2003. Techniques to identify themes. 2003. *Field Methods* 15(1): 85–109.

Debriefing

Schoepfle, G. Mark and Oswald Werner. 1999. Ethnographic debriefing. *Field Methods* 11(2): 158–165.

Interviewing

Seidman, Irving. 1991. Technique isn't everything, but it is a lot. In *Interviewing as Qualitative Research: A Guide for Researchers in Education and the Social Sciences*, edited by Irving Seidman, 56–71. New York: Teachers College Press.

Spradley, James. 2002. Asking descriptive questions. In *Qualitative Approaches to Criminal Justice: Perspectives from the Field*, edited by Mark Pogrebin, 44–53. Thousand Oaks, CA: Sage Publishing.

Turner, Daniel W. 2010. Qualitative interview design: A practical guide for novice investigators. *The Qualitative Report* 15(3): 754–760.

Index